"A full picture about one of the most important developments in Lincoln's life: the successful effort to acquire the Republican presidential nomination in Chicago in 1860. Jay Miner's handling of the material, astute analysis of the activities of the 'Lincoln men' at the convention, and good understanding of the significance of the work going on behind the scenes will make this book an invaluable contribution toward understanding how Lincoln became president."

—Dr. Phillip C. Stone
Founder, Lincoln Society of Virginia

HON. ABRAHAM LINCOLN.
"OUR NEXT PRESIDENT".

Lincoln's First Nomination

Champagne, Deals, & Dirty Tricks

Jay C. Miner

History4All, Inc.
Fairfax, Virginia

Lincoln's First Nomination

Champagne, Deals, & Dirty Tricks

Jay C. Miner

© 2008 by Jay C. Miner

Published by History4All, Inc.
Post Office Box 1126
Fairfax, Virginia 22038
www.history4all.net

ISBN 978-1-934285-06-0
Library of Congress Control Number: 2008933194

Printed in the United States of America
First Edition
First Printing, August 2008

Page Design and Copyediting: Marion B. Meany, Fairfax, Virginia.
Compositing and Manufacturing: Allen Wayne Ltd., Chantilly, Virginia.
Cover Design: Baldersons Inc., Chantilly, Virginia.

Contents

Introduction

A Universe in Itself

Theodore H. White, in *The Making of the President 1960*, accurately and definitively described the phenomenon of the political convention: "Every convention is a universe in itself, with its own strange centers of gravity, its own fresh heroes and fools, its own resolution of pressures and forces, its own irrecapturable mood to stage and place."[1]

What was true in 1960 Los Angeles was true a century earlier in Chicago, where the then-new Republican Party nominated Abraham Lincoln for president. The Republican Convention of 1860 was, indeed, a universe in itself: a short-lived universe whose life cycle was measured in days, hours, and minutes rather than the weeks, months, and years of current presidential campaigns. For the few precious days of its existence, the nation's attention was riveted on the political universe's epicenter, Chicago. The electorate anxiously waited for this political drama to play out. The decision made then in Chicago has profoundly affected the course of American history.

The activities of a political convention are "far too fluid and hysterical a phenomenon for exact history," said historian Arthur M. Schlesinger, Jr. "Everything happens at once and everywhere, and everything changes too quickly. People talk too much, smoke too much, rush too much and sleep too little. Fatigue tightens nerves and produces susceptibility to rumor and panic. No one can see a convention whole. And no one can remember it with precision later, partly because it is so hard to reconstruct the sequence of events and partly because people always say and do things they wish to forget. At the time it is all a confusion; in retrospect it is all a blur."[2] Certain facts, however, are known, reported by reputable observers.

As presidential historian and journalist Joseph Bucklin Bishop wrote:

> The [1860] convention marked an epoch in the history of such bodies. It was the first of the great modern convention assemblages, which are at once the most impressive and the most tumultuous in the world. It was the first to have a special building erected for its use, and the first to bring telegraph wires and instruments into the building itself. It was the first, also, to admit the general public in large numbers . . .[3]

The Republican Convention of 1860 had it all: champagne and cigars, dirty tricks, marching bands, parades, political wheeling and dealing, old-fashioned horse-trading, a sprinkling of sex, smoke-filled rooms, and for one particular delegate, sweet, sweet political revenge.

Some of the most influential public figures of the time were either at the 1860 convention or cast their shadows, sometimes posthumously, on the event: Henry Clay, Daniel Webster, Horace Greeley, John Brown, and Stephen A. Douglas. Most important, a man who wasn't physically there, Abraham Lincoln, had laid the foundation for the victory that his friends and supporters achieved for him at Chicago.

And it nearly didn't happen! All the clever planning in the world can be undone by a circumstance that is for one candidate good fortune, for his opponent, disaster.

Chapter 1

A History of Compromise

The differences between life in the "good old days" of 1860 when Lincoln walked the political landscape and life in the 21st century, in terms of living conditions and physical comforts, are countless. The differences between 1860 politics and the politics of today are equally as imposing. There were then no exploratory committees formed to investigate presidential possibilities. Potential candidates did not square off in presidential primaries to demonstrate their ability to attract votes. The quadrennial winter visit to New Hampshire by presidential wannabes was decades away. Instead, candidate selection was the result of political bargaining or political intrigue. It was usually conducted in smoke-filled back rooms where the co-conspirators, in low, muted voices, surreptitiously planned and schemed. A candidate's political success in 1860, first and foremost, depended on the strength and determination of his party.

In addition, politics in the 21st century is decidedly more complicated, complex, and expensive. For instance, in 1860, an aspirant did not have to raise large sums of money in order to be a player in the high-stakes game of presidential politics. Nor did presidential hopefuls have professional staffs to focus on issues or direct their activities. Abraham Lincoln was not a wealthy man and he did his own research, wrote and delivered his own speeches. While he at times asked others for their opinions, he held his own counsel and very rarely yielded to their advice.[4]

National conventions nowadays, however, through changes in party nominating procedures and the increased importance of the primary results, have become occasions for formalizing candidate choices already made and for drumming up partisan enthusiasm. They are pale echoes of earlier events, such as the convention of 1860, which had high drama and a paramount issue.

In 1860, while there were then standing questions about free homesteads, tariff revision, internal improvements, and the building of a Pacific railroad, the sole issue that stirred the nation, and that to a boiling point, was the future of slavery. It was an issue that candidate-to-be Lincoln had studied, understood, and debated extensively.

The prevalent position of the North was to prevent slavery from spreading into the new territories, and the South wanted its "peculiar institution," as abolitionists dubbed it, protected as a guaranteed constitutional right.

The issue was so divisive that it split churches, political parties, and families. In the first half of the 1800s, when the slavery issue had erupted and inflamed the nation, the political leaders had fallen back on the same legislative stock-in-trade used since the formation of the union: accommodation. To avoid head-to-head confrontation, the leaders brokered a bipartisan compromise, which temporarily smoothed over the symptoms but offered no true cure for the cancerous malignancy, the disease of human bondage.

Until 1850, compromise was a tried-and-true American homeopathic remedy, a quick fix that helped maintain the status quo between the free states and the slave states. Although each political fix was legislatively devised to last indefinitely, the nation quickly found out "indefinitely" was never more than a year or two.

The Missouri Compromise of 1820 was one of the major accommodations made between the anti- and proslavery factions. As Lincoln explained, in one of his many debates on the issue, the Missouri Compromise provided a plan by which states entering the union would be designated slave or free: "Missouri might come into the Union *with* slavery, but that in all the remaining part of the territory purchased of France, which lies north of 36 degrees and

30 minutes north latitude, slavery should never be permitted."[5] That plan had prevailed until 1850 when another compromise was needed to deal with new territories obtained by the U.S. after war with Mexico.

The resulting compromise brought California into the Union as a free state, preserved slave ownership in the nation's capital, and strengthened the fugitive slave law. This came about primarily through the efforts of two of the most revered politicians of their time. Senator Henry Clay, Kentucky, who had been instrumental in brokering the Missouri Compromise, came out of retirement and joined forces with Senator Daniel Webster, Massachusetts, for their last hurrah on the national stage.

The passage of the 1850 Compromise failed to ease sectional tensions as its sponsors and supporters had envisaged. Its implementation immediately reignited the slavery agitation and inflamed the country. The Compromise marked the beginning of the end of the South's peculiar institution.

With the new legislative equation favoring the free states (16 free to 15 slave) and the pendulum beginning to swing in favor of the North, the South officially became a minority. Consequently, over the next decade, the South's idle threat to secede became a viable political option when the Democratic Party claimed that it had yielded ground until it had "come at last to points beyond which we can yield no further."[6]

The seeds of civil war, which had been sown over the years since the nation's independence and had been held in check by disingenuous legislative subterfuge, now broke through the surface and began to grow and flourish. Hereafter, the slavery issue would never return to political dormancy. The gulf between the two regions became too wide to be bridged by compromise. The only question to be answered was not if, but when, hostilities would replace rhetoric.

Lincoln, too, believed that "the day of compromise has passed. These two great ideas [slavery and freedom] have been kept apart only by the most artful means. They are like two wild beasts in sight of each other, but chained and held apart. Some day these deadly antagonists will one or the other break their bonds and then the question will be settled."[7]

While not trying to oversimplify the slavery issue as it affected the nation in the 1850s, there were basically three points of view: that of those who wanted slavery; that of those who wanted it abolished; and that of those who wanted to bridge the gap. Abraham Lincoln fell into the last category. He was against the extension of slavery but would not interfere with it in the states where it existed.

Chapter 2

Lincoln's Future Opponent

The passage of the Kansas-Nebraska Act had prompted Lincoln's remarks on the slavery issue. The author of the bill was Senator Stephen A. Douglas of Illinois, and his motives were colored by his thirst for the presidency. One of the most powerful men in America and Lincoln's future rival for the presidency, Douglas was known as the Little Giant, small in stature but large in intellect.

To accomplish his presidential aspirations, Douglas devised a plan he believed would "bridge the gap" and win him support in both the North and South. In 1854, as chairman of the Senate's powerful Committee on Territories, he introduced the Kansas-Nebraska Act, aimed at organizing the Kansas and Nebraska territories and setting out his "popular sovereignty" concept. This concept held that, since all political power resided in the people, it was the people, not the federal government, who should decide the question of slavery in their own territory. The 1854 act made the settlers in the territories "free to choose whether they would have slavery as an institution or not."[8] They could vote it up or down. Under the Kansas-Nebraska Act provisions, the Missouri Compromise prohibition of slavery north of 36° 30' latitude was repealed.

As soon as the bill was introduced, it created a firestorm of rage throughout the North. It inflamed the slave controversy more than ever. Northerners characterized the bill as a slaveholder's plot and the question of slavery again resonated on every tongue. Because more new territory was opening north of the Mason and Dixon Line

Stephen A. Douglas

than south of it, the measure was popular in the South. However, it was most vigorously condemned everywhere in the North where "Douglas was roundly denounced as a traitor, a Judas Iscariot" and "he was actually presented with 'thirty pieces of silver' by a woman's organization in Ohio."[9] Whereas earlier disruptions over slavery were confined to radicals and extremists, now the silent majority—the conservatives and moderates—raised their collective voices and eagerly joined in the fight. The goal of stopping the spread of slavery advanced and was fast becoming a principle "to die for."

The Kansas-Nebraska Act became law in May 1854. Because it was surrounded by free states, Nebraska became a free state. Kansas, on the other hand, adjoined two slave states, Missouri and Arkansas, and became a battleground. It was the first head-to-head confrontation pitting those who would spread slavery against the abolitionists. "The stories of raids, election frauds, murders, and other crimes were moving eastward with marked rapidity. These outbursts of frontier lawlessness, led and sanctioned by the avowed proslavery element, were not only stirring up the Abolitionists to fever heat, but touching the hearts of humanity in general."[10]

The antislavery forces in the North organized settlers, sent them to Kansas, and supplied them with the necessaries. The necessaries included rifles and ammunition, shipped in containers labeled "Bibles" and "Hardware."[11] The rifles one abolitionist-preacher, Henry Ward Beecher, sent became known as Beecher's Bibles.[12] In Kansas, to the antislavery forces, biblical scripture was delivered not only from the pulpit but in lead shots.

As the North organized and sent settlers into Kansas, the South became aroused. Not only did proslavery emigrants move into the territory through Missouri, but slave owners in Missouri formed guerilla organizations and supplied them with guns and whiskey, always a lethal combination.[13] To the guerillas, two shots were better than one, especially if the first was a shot of John Barleycorn and the second a shot at an abolitionist settler.

Here, too, is when the nation first heard of John Brown of Ossawatomie. In 1856, after proslavery forces attacked and sacked

Lawrence, Kansas, Brown headed a reprisal group and slaughtered five proslavery colonists living near Pottawatomie Creek.[14] The confrontation of North and South in Kansas was a dress rehearsal and preview of the bloody rebellion to come.

When Douglas returned to his home state from the East to defend his role in the passage of the Kansas-Nebraska Act, he found the citizens in an uproar. He claimed he was able to go from Boston to Chicago by the light of his burning effigies.[15] Church bells tolled in protest against him. Flags were lowered to half-mast. At a gathering in Chicago, Douglas tried to explain his position but the crowd shouted him down and drowned out all his attempts to speak. Douglas, a rough-and-ready fighter determined to tell his side, became defiant and announced he would stay till morning. The crowd took the challenge and screamed they would not go home before morning. It was the Little Giant against the people, and both sides stubbornly dug in their heels. Shortly after midnight, Douglas broke the stalemate and roared to the crowd, "Abolitionists of Chicago! It is now Sunday morning—I'll go to church and you may go to hell!" He took his leave.[16]

Unfortunately for Douglas, another man from Illinois opposed him and his popular sovereignty concept and the Kansas-Nebraska Act. That man was Abraham Lincoln. After his term in Congress ended in 1849, and failing to be appointed to a federal position, Lincoln had returned to Springfield and "applied himself with unremitting assiduity to the practice of law,"[17] fast becoming a leading lawyer in Illinois. The introduction of the legislation rekindled his passion for politics. "He saw in the effort of Douglas a movement of the South, not only to save slavery but to advance it" and "believed this would tend to undermine the very principles of the Declaration of Independence."[18] Lincoln rejoined the fight against the extension of slavery, determined to participate in finding the way the nation would go in solving the slavery dilemma. Lincoln's unfailing opposition to Douglas earned him fame and elevated him to the national stage. From that time forward, whenever Douglas advocated, Lincoln remonstrated.

Chapter 3

Birth of the Republican Party

When none of the established political parties (Whigs, Know Nothings, or Democrats) focused on the long-range impact of slavery or pressed for a plan on how to deal with the issue, party loyalty crumbled. Party members began searching for political alignments that expressed their beliefs, i.e., an organization that was issue-oriented rather than party-oriented. Antislavery Democrats and antislavery Whigs, long-time political enemies who intensely distrusted one another, felt themselves drawn together by a common, overpowering conviction to stop the expansion of slavery. Calls for a new organization echoed throughout the North, Thus, in 1854 in Michigan, the Republican Party came into existence.[19] This party would soon become a home to Abraham Lincoln, who in 1854 was a Whig.

Without doubt, the birth of the new party, according to one author, "was a revolutionary rising against the status quo of human bondage."[20] Its membership consisted not only of former Whigs and Democrats, but also abolitionists, free soilers,[21] protectionists and free traders, foreign-born citizens and Know Nothings. The new party "appealed so strongly to idealistic young men and had drawn so heavily upon the best Whig and free-soil Democratic talent that it was rich in ability," according to historian Allan Nevins. It soon spread to other states.[22] These newcomers brought ideas and ambitions which would profoundly change political life in the United States.

One of the factions forming the new party, the Know Nothings, was a unique group that deserves attention because of the role it would play in the political drama that unfolded in Chicago. The Know Nothings, quite possibly the first WASP (White Anglo-Saxon Protestant) combination, came into existence primarily as a nativist response to the massive immigration of Catholics from Ireland and Germany during the 1840s. The newcomers' five-year naturalization period had ended and they had now begun to vote. The Know Nothings' main concern was focused on opposing foreigners rather than slavery and, before becoming a bona fide political party, the Know Nothings operated as a secret order with passwords and hand grips. When anyone asked a member about his organization, the reply was, "I know nothing." Although the members of the new party called themselves the American Party, outsiders called them Know Nothings.[23]

The constitution of its party in Connecticut left no doubts about its primary purpose:

> Its object shall be to resist the insidious policy of the Church of Rome, and all other foreign influences against the institutions of our country, by placing in all offices in the gift of the people, whether by election or appointment, none but native-born Protestant citizens.[24]

When in power the Know Nothings did whatever they could to put obstacles in the paths of foreign-born citizens. Some states considered proposals increasing the residency requirements for naturalization. In Connecticut, a proposal was made to extend the term to 21 years.[25] However, while the group was against all foreigners, it had no resolution for the slavery question, and no sooner had it became an open political entity than it began to lose its political clout and soon became a faction within the larger Republican Party.

Abraham Lincoln, who had not run for office since his term as a U.S. congressman ended in 1849, came out of hibernation in 1854. He made, in 1855, the first of his two unsuccessful tries for a seat in the U.S. Senate. He was then still a Whig and, in order for him to be elected by the Illinois legislature, would require a coalition of Whigs, abolitionists, and anti-Nebraska Democrats. Although Lincoln received the most votes on the first ballot, he ultimately lost the election. He wrote to a friend and explained the particulars of his loss:

> I began with 44 votes, Shields 41, and Trumbull 5,—yet Trumbull was elected. In fact 47 different members voted for me,—getting three new ones on the second ballot, and losing four old ones. How came my 47 to yield to Trumbull's 5? It was Governor Matteson's work. He has been secretly a candidate ever since (before, even) the fall election.

Matteson's support was pro-Nebraska and his impending victory caused Lincoln to turn his support to the Democrat, Lyman Trumbull. Wrote Lincoln:

> I became satisfied that if we could prevent Matteson's election one or two ballots more, we could not possibly do so a single ballot after my friends should begin to return to me from Trumbull. So I determined to strike at once, and accordingly advised my remaining friends, to go for him [Trumbull], which they did and elected him on the tenth ballot.[26]

Two of the original five Trumbull supporters were Norman Judd and John Palmer, both anti-Nebraska Democrats. Although they vigorously opposed Lincoln's election to the U.S. Senate in 1855 and forced him to throw his support to anti-Nebraska Democrat Trumbull, these men (as well as the other three) later became true Lincoln men and played prominent roles in Lincoln's successful run for the Republican presidential nomination in 1860.[27]

Soon, the slavery conflict spilled over into the halls of Congress. In May 1856, Senator Charles Sumner of Massachusetts, speaking in the Senate in favor of admitting Kansas into the Union as a free state, made some remarks about Senator Andrew Pickens Butler of South Carolina. Shortly after the Senate adjourned and while Sumner was sitting at his desk, Congressman Preston Brooks, Senator Butler's nephew, fell on him with a cane, knocked him

Lyman Trumbull

down under his desk, and beat him so severely that he was carried off bleeding and insensible.[28] While Sumner recuperated, his Senate seat would remain vacant for three years, "a silent but eloquent reminder that violence had threatened the legislative process in America."[29]

While the attack inflamed the North, it was called a "handsome drubbing" by the *Edgefield (South Carolina) Advertiser* in an article titled "Hit Him Again." The article read, "The beating is said by all the reporters to have been a thorough one. Some say he received 55 stripes; yet we very much doubt if the Captain cared to exceed the legal number of 39, usually applied to scamps."[30]

Amid the sectional conflict caused by slavery, the Republican Party came into existence in Illinois at Bloomington on May 29, 1856. Lincoln began to take an active part in organizing the new party. He attended a gathering of anti-Nebraska editors in February and a call was issued throughout the state for a mass convention. Men who had formerly been bitter antagonists now joined together to resist slavery extension.[31] Lincoln and his law partner, William Herndon, attended the Illinois Republican convention and joined the party, as did the two former Democrats, Norman Judd and John Palmer. All in attendance were aware they were "forming a new political party on the premise that slavery must be restricted until it would eventually die out in the United States."[32]

The convention gave birth to "the confederated factions of the Illinois Republicans." From its birth the factions clashed violently: "The conservative Free Soilers reviled the rabid Abolitionists; the large foreign-born German group glared at the former Know-Nothings; the old-line Whigs scorned the Democrats who had lately become Republicans."[33]

The convention adopted a strong anti-Nebraska platform and, when its official business was over, Lincoln, among others, was called on to speak. He delivered such a speech that "no one who heard it will ever forget the effect it produced."[34] One reporter covering the convention wrote:

For an hour and a half he held the assembly spellbound by the power of his argument, the intense irony of his invective, and the deep earnestness and fervid brilliancy of his eloquence.[35]

At one point in the speech Lincoln galvanized the crowd when he raised his arms toward the ceiling and shouted, "We do not intend to dissolve the Union, nor do we intend to let you dissolve it."[36]

His law partner, William Herndon, wrote that he took notes for about the first 15 minutes but because of the power of the speech and the magic of Lincoln's ideas, he "threw pen and paper away and lived only in the inspiration of the hour."[37] Because no record of the speech was ever made it became known as Lincoln's "Lost Speech."

Lincoln's message thrust him into a party leadership position, providing his listeners with the first glimpse of the qualities that would ultimately make him the icon he is today and quite possibly put "Lincoln on the track for the presidency."[38]

The new Republican Party met in Philadelphia from June 17 to 19, 1856, and, at its first national convention, nominated John C. Fremont of California for president and William Dayton of New Jersey for vice president. Although he did not attend the convention, Lincoln was named for vice president by Amos Tuck of New Hampshire and received 100 votes.[39] Tuck also came to the 1860 Republican Convention in Chicago, again a delegate from New Hampshire and still a Lincoln friend and admirer.

When the Democrats met in 1856 to nominate a candidate, Senator Stephen A. Douglas was making his first serious run at the Democratic nomination. He was, however, unsuccessful. After 17 ballots, the Democrats chose James Buchanan of Pennsylvania for president and John S. Breckinridge of Kentucky for vice president. Buchanan was the victor in November, winning 14 slave states and 4 free states. Fremont won 11 free states. The Whig Party, in its last national election, nominated Millard Fillmore for president and he won one free state.

William H. Herndon

On March 6, 1857, two days after Buchanan was sworn in as president, the Supreme Court handed down the *Dred Scott* decision, written by Chief Justice Roger B. Taney, a slaveholder. Dred Scott, a slave, claimed that because he was transported by his master from Missouri, a slave state, into Illinois and the territory north of the latitude 36° 30' north, and then four years later transported back to Missouri, his extended stay in the free territory made him free. The Court denied his claim on the grounds that a slave is property and a property right is protected by the Constitution from dissolution except through due process of law.[40]

The Court went even further and, "proceeding with what lawyers call *obiter dictum*," declared that no act of Congress (or a territorial legislature) can constitutionally deprive a slave master of his property.[41] With a stroke of the supreme judicial pen, any act, congressional or territorial, banning slavery was unconstitutional. The South could claim that inasmuch as Congress had no right to deprive citizens of their property, slavery and the slave trade were lawful throughout the nation.

Chapter 4

The Great Debates

In 1858, the battleground over the extension of slavery came to Illinois when Senator Douglas sought reelection to the Senate. Abraham Lincoln was chosen as his Republican opponent. In his acceptance speech, Lincoln staked out a controversial position over the objections of some of his supporters. To express his stand on the slavery issue, he "wanted to use some universally known figure expressed in simple language . . . that may strike home to the minds of men in order to raise them up to the peril of the times."[42] He found it in the Bible. In his speech, Lincoln attacked slavery but not slaveholders, and borrowed from scripture that a "house divided against itself cannot stand" and added "this government cannot endure permanently half slave and half free."[43]

The ensuing campaign produced the seven Lincoln-Douglas debates where the issue of slavery was openly debated for the first time in America. It was also the first time newspapers printed a verbatim account of each debate. The format of the debates was simple. One candidate would open (they alternated openings) and speak for an hour, the other candidate would then speak for 90 minutes, then the first would have 30 minutes in rebuttal.[44]

The setting of the Lincoln-Douglas debates was "on sun-baked courthouse squares amid a circle of farmers' buggies, galluses, and stovepipe hats."[45] The crowds numbered in the thousands. Many traveled for days to attend. They stood for hours, listening and cheering their favorite as the two candidates slugged it out, toe to toe, in oratorical battle over the one divisive issue of the day. One spectator, who attended the Quincy, Illinois, debate between the two political warriors, wrote that the spectacle reminded him "of two armies in battle array, standing still to see their two principal champions fight out the contested cause between the lines in single combat."[46]

A few points to remember: In the 1850s, in North and South, politics was the one and only national pastime and it did not have to compete with other forms of entertainment—movies, television and sporting events—for supremacy. When the people attended a political event, they expected to be entertained, and the Lincoln-Douglas debates provided the nation with seven political Super Bowls.

These debates showcased men who were masters and not servants of their oratorical powers. Lincoln had no peers in stump speaking.[47] Douglas was no slouch either, and both genuinely loved the give and take of a debate. The two antagonists could not have been more dissimilar:

> When they sat side by side, there was a difference of four inches in their height; and when standing together, Abe towered fourteen inches above Steve, who was only five feet two.[48]

Lincoln was normally attired in ill-fitting clothing that was rumpled and needing a pressing. Douglas, square-shouldered and broad-chested with a massive head upon a strong neck, was the picture of sartorial splendor in his tailor-made garb.

While on stage, both combatants had their own particular styles that fit their distinct personalities and neither would ever put the people in the front rows to sleep. Lincoln would gesture with his arms and, when he wanted to emphasize a point and liven up his performance, would bend his knees and body with a sudden downward jerk, then shoot up again onto his tiptoes.[49] Douglas was entertaining, too. While listening to Lincoln's speech, he occasionally displayed a contemptuous smile and when he rose, the tough parliamentary gladiator tossed his mane with an air of overbearing superiority. If it had been possible, the Little Giant would have loved to pass off his antagonist as the Tall Dwarf.[50]

Second, there were no loudspeakers. A candidate's raised voice was the only amplification available to deliver his message to the far reaches of the audience. The larger the crowd the greater the vocal effort. Lincoln's voice was rather "high-keyed," and while "apt to turn into a shrill treble in moments of excitement," on the whole, "it had an exceedingly penetrating, far-reaching quality."[51] In contrast, Douglas's voice was "a strong baritone," and "gave forth a hoarse and rough, at times even something like a barking, sound."[52] When the debates were over, Douglas's voice was so hoarse he could hardly be heard.

What would it have been like to have met Lincoln in person during this time? Wisconsin's Carl Schurz described meeting with Lincoln on the eve of the Quincy, Illinois, debate:

> I must confess that I was somewhat startled by his appearance. There he stood, overtopping by several inches all those surrounding him. Although measuring something over six feet myself, I had, standing quite near to him, to throw my head backward in order to look into his eyes. That swarthy face with its strong features, its deep furrows, and its benignant, melancholy eyes . . .

> On his head he wore a somewhat battered "stove-pipe" hat. His neck emerged, long and sinewy, from a white collar turned down over a thin black necktie. His lank, ungainly body was clad in a rusty black dress coat with sleeves that should have been longer; but his arms appeared so long that the sleeves of a "store" coat could hardly be expected to cover them all the way down to the wrists. His black trousers, too, permitted a very full view of his large feet. On his left arm he carried a gray woolen shawl, which evidently served him for an overcoat in chilly weather. His left hand held a cotton umbrella of the bulging kind, and also a black satchel that bore the marks of long and hard usage. His right [hand] he had kept free for handshaking, of which there was no end until everybody in the car seemed to be satisfied.[53]

In the second debate, at Freeport, Lincoln "made what is generally accepted as his greatest political stroke." He asked Douglas whether there was a legal way to keep slavery out of a territory. It was a loaded question and "intended to commit Douglas unqualifiedly for or against the principle of the *Dred Scott* decision, which held that neither Congress nor a territorial legislature could prohibit slavery in the territories."[54] Douglas, placed squarely between the proverbial rock and the hard place, had to weigh his response in terms of his chances for reelection, on the one hand, against, on the other, his thirst for the presidency. Lofty principles became intertwined with practical politics. Douglas was forced to make the supreme political choice. A "no" answer would endear him to the South but probably undermine his reelection and, unless he held his Senate seat, the presidency would forever be a dream. A "yes" answer would help him retain his Senate seat but would be the equivalent of committing political suicide in the South. Douglas, if anything, was a pragmatic politician who took care of first things first, and getting reelected was his first priority in 1858. His answer, made in the heat of battle, was yes, that while the *Dred Scott* decision prevents the outlawing of slavery, slavery could be kept out of a territory if there were no local black codes to protect property. (Local black codes were laws pertaining to the recapture of runaway slaves.)

While Douglas's response satisfied his Illinois constituents, it gave him the mark of Cain in the South. When reelected, Douglas shifted his priorities to his presidential dream and endeavored to regain Southern support. He had two years to repair the damage caused by his answer and give it a favorable southern spin. Little did he know that he had lost the support of the South forever.

What occurred at the debates was national news and the whole nation watched with interest. If they could not be there in person to see the battle of the giants, they wanted to be able to read a full account of the proceedings. At the Freeport debate, for instance, Lincoln had the opening and closing, and when he rose from his chair to begin to address the crowd of 15,000 people, a voice cried out from the back of the crowd, "Hold on, Lincoln, you can't speak yet. Hitt isn't here and there is no use of your speaking unless the *Tribune* has a report." Robert R. Hitt was a shorthand expert who had been employed by the *Chicago Press and Tribune* to transcribe the debates word for word. Once located, Hitt was lifted into the air and propelled onto the platform and the debate began.[55]

It was a hard-fought contest between two giants who were "both in the full maturity of their physical and intellectual powers. Douglas was 45 years old, and Lincoln was 49."[56] Neither gave nor expected quarter and the match was about equal. "Unbiased hearers said that when Douglas spoke they felt sorry for Lincoln, and when Lincoln spoke they felt sorry for Douglas."[57] On election day, Lincoln received 4,144 more votes than Douglas, but Douglas won the election.[58] In 1858, U.S. senators were elected by the state legislatures and in Illinois the Democrats had an eight vote advantage over the Republicans, 54 to 46.[59] (All Democratic legislators voted for Douglas.)

In fairness to Douglas, in the campaign he had to take on Lincoln and also fight the national Democratic Party. Because Douglas had split with the Buchanan administration over Kansas, the administration fielded a candidate in an attempt to siphon votes away from him and possibly defeat him. The official vote: Republicans, 126,084; Douglas Democrats, 121,940; Buchanan Democrats, 5,091.[60] If Douglas had in fact received the united Democratic vote (121,940 + 5,091 = 127,031), he would have won the popular vote by less than a thousand votes—a real cliffhanger, but he would have been the winner over Lincoln in the popular vote, as well.

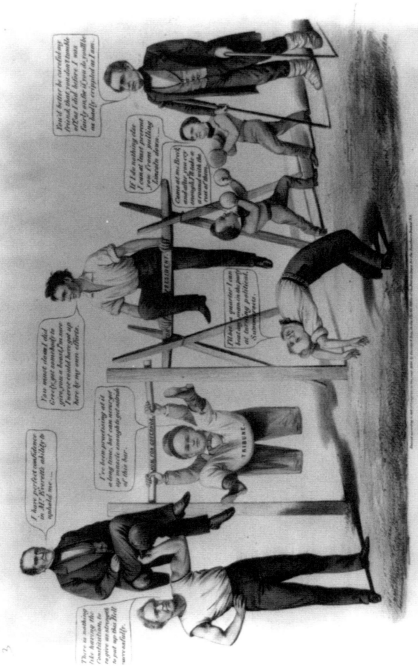

THE POLITICAL GYMNASIUM.

Chapter 5

Exploring Presidential Possibilities

Before the dust had settled in his election loss to Douglas in 1858, Lincoln realized he had hit political gold in the debates: national recognition. He had struck a responsive chord in all Republicans on the one divisive issue of the day. In a letter to a friend, Lincoln expressed what it had meant to him to challenge Douglas and participate in the great debates:

> I am glad I made the late race. It gave me a hearing on the great and durable question of the age, which I could have had in no other way; and . . . I believe I have made some marks, which will tell for the cause of civil liberty long after I am gone.[61]

It was probably during the debates that the presidency first glimmered in his imagination and he began to nurture and enhance his image.

One Illinois supporter, Jesse Fell,[62] believed that Lincoln's efforts in the campaign demonstrated that Illinois had two giants: Douglas, the little one who was well known throughout the nation, and Lincoln, the big one who was little known outside of Illinois. Fell, a native of Pennsylvania, solicited Lincoln for a short biography which, coupled with facts from Lincoln's public life Fell would add, would be circulated in Pennsylvania in a "well-considered, well-written newspaper article, telling the people who you are, and what you have done."[63] Fell had the decided impression that "if

Lincoln's personal history and his speeches on the slavery question were brought before the public, . . . Lincoln could become a serious presidential contender."[64]

Fell also presented a feasible scenario for Lincoln to capture the nomination when he described the ideal Republican candidate in the next presidential election: "What the Republican Party wants, to insure success in 1860, is a man of popular origin, of acknowledged ability, committed against slavery aggressions, who has no record to defend, and no radicalism of an offensive character. . . ."[65]

Although Lincoln failed to provide the requested biography until December 1859, nearly 14 months after Fell's request, his political motor was never idle. The desire to elevate himself was the primary driving force in Lincoln. He had a longing for political recognition and success. He was determined to turn the setback of his defeat into an opportunity for national office.

His interest in politics was national rather than gubernatorial. Although he had served a term in the House of Representatives he had no desire to return. Lincoln's national office of choice was the Senate. He was always running for the next Senate opening—in 1855 and again in 1858—and he admitted to Norman Judd in December 1859 that he would rather be in the Senate than be president.[66] Although there would be a Senate seat open in Illinois in 1860, it was currently held by a fellow Republican, Lyman Trumbull, the former anti-Nebraska Democrat who had beaten him in 1855, and Lincoln had vowed not to oppose him.[67] The next Senate race possible for Lincoln would be in 1864, but in 1860 there would be two other national job openings: president and vice president. He had nothing to lose by going after either one. Even if he failed to be nominated for either office and the Republicans won the White House in 1860, he could be appointed to a cabinet position in the new administration.

To make a successful run for national office, Lincoln knew he would have to orchestrate his own campaign over the next 18 months and win new political friends throughout the North while not alienating any wing of the Republican Party. In addition, in order to have a reasonable chance for the nomination, it was imperative that the Illinois state party rally round his candidacy. If he failed to accomplish all three objectives, national office would be elusive. This was a formidable undertaking, but for Lincoln, a political genius who was able to play the game of politics to perfection, a piece of cake.

While working toward these objectives, he had to keep a low political profile as a potential candidate. The nominating convention was more than a year away and, rather than having to undergo intense scrutiny from potential rivals and their supporters, he wanted to remain a noncandidate until the time was most propitious. He deflected all attempts to have his name placed in contention for president. When a group of lawyer-politicians met on January 6, 1859, and wanted to explore establishing a Lincoln-for-president movement, Lincoln, knowing any movement at this time could work against him, wisely protested and the effort died on the vine.[68] Later, when Thomas Pickett, in a letter dated April 13, 1859, asked to confer with him about announcing his candidacy,[69] Lincoln responded three days later that while he was flattered he did not think himself fit for the presidency.[70]

His strategy worked to perfection. He had been so successful in hiding his true motives that when a list of 21 presidential contenders was published in 1859, his name did not appear on it. Nor did his name appear in a list of 34 men with presidential qualifications that was published in Philadelphia in early 1860.[71]

Nevertheless, Lincoln had to stay visible, and that meant he had to stay in print. One way to stay in print and to keep his name and message before the public was to get his debates with Douglas published. Lincoln corresponded with his newspaper friends, requesting they send him copies of the debates for his scrapbook.[72] Once his scrapbook was complete he put out feelers to publishers in Springfield to see if he could generate interest in getting them published. He was, however, unsuccessful at first, proving that "a prophet is not without honor, save in his own country."[73]

Thanks to the debates, Lincoln was asked for his autograph and his opinion on national affairs and received invitations to speak from more and more groups throughout the North. He knew his speeches had the power to ignite the imagination and would generate favorable publicity in the North. More important, he knew his speeches would, in all likelihood, be the lead story in all Republican newspapers in the land, and in some instances, the speeches would be printed in their entirety. With that in mind, Lincoln decided to accept some speaking invitations. He would take his one-man show on the road, to battle for the righteousness of the Republican cause and to help get Republican candidates elected.

During 1859, Lincoln traveled 4,000 miles to deliver 23 political speeches in Iowa, Ohio, Indiana, Wisconsin, and Kansas.[74] In each arena, he sought the party leaders and the ones who controlled party politics. He was well aware the personal political contacts he made during this time were essential to his run for the nomination.

Indirectly, Senator Douglas helped shape and promote Lincoln's crystallizing political aspirations. Thanks to the debates, Lincoln had officially become the Giant Killer. "Throughout the year 1859 politicians and newspapers came to look upon Lincoln as the one antagonist who could at all times be relied on to answer and refute the Douglas arguments."[75] Consequently, whenever Douglas visited a state, or scheduled a visit to stump for Democrats, the Republicans immediately called for Abe the Giant Killer to come to the rescue and spearhead the Republican counterattack. Lincoln responded to one such call from Ohio Republicans to "head off the little gentleman"[76] and in September 1859 made four Ohio speeches, at Cincinnati, Columbus, Dayton, and Hamilton, all before thousands of people. On the way back to Springfield, he made a stopover at Indianapolis to deliver an address.[77]

When the elections were held in Ohio in October, the Republican Party increased its majority in the state legislature, winning 25 of 35 Senate seats and 64 of 104 House seats.[78] They were so thankful for Lincoln's efforts they took steps to have his debates with Douglas published in book form. The book came out shortly before the Republican Convention of 1860 and "thirty thousand copies of the book were rapidly sold."[79]

Lincoln, also, in a letter dated December 20, 1859, fulfilled the earlier request of Jesse Fell to provide him with a short biography: "Here is the little sketch, as you requested. There is not much of it, for the reason, I suppose, that there is not much of me."[80]

As of December 20, 1859, in less than 600 words, Lincoln modestly sized up his qualifications for the nation's highest office:

I was born February 12, 1809, in Hardin County, Kentucky. My parents were both born in Virginia, of undistinguished families— second families, perhaps I should say. My mother, who died in my tenth year, was of a family of the name Hanks, some of whom now reside in Adams, and others in Macon County, Illinois. My paternal grandfather, Abraham Lincoln, emigrated from Rockingham County, Virginia, to Kentucky about 1781 or 1782, where a year or two later he was killed by the Indians, not in battle, but by stealth, when he was laboring to open a farm in the forest. His ancestors, who were Quakers, went to Virginia from Berks County, Pennsylvania. An effort to identify them with the New England family of the same name ended in nothing more definite than a similarity of Christian names in both families, such as Enoch, Levi, Mordecai, Solomon, Abraham, and the like.

My father, at the death of his father, was but six years of age, and he grew up literally without education. He removed from Kentucky to what is now Spencer County, Indiana, in my eighth year. We reached our new home about the time the State came into the Union. It was a wild region, with many bears and other wild animals still in the woods. There I grew up. There were some schools, so called, but no qualification was ever required of a teacher beyond "readin,' writin,' and cipherin'" to the rule of three. If a straggler supposed to understand Latin happened to sojourn in the neighborhood, he was looked upon as a wizard. There was absolutely nothing to excite ambition for education. Of course, when I came of age I did not know much. Still, somehow, I could read, write and cipher to the rule of three, but that was all. I have not been to school since. The little advance I now have upon this store of education, I have picked up from time to time under the pressure of necessity.

I was raised to farm work, which I continued till I was 22. At 22 I came to Illinois, Macon County. Then I got to New Salem, at that time in Sangamon, now in Menard County, where I remained a year as sort of clerk in a store. Then came the Black Hawk war;

and I was elected a captain of volunteers, a success which gave me more pleasure than any I have had since. I went the campaign, was elated, ran for the legislature the same year (1832), and was beaten—the only time I ever have been beaten by the people. The next and three succeeding biennial elections I was elected to the legislature. I was not a candidate afterward. During this legislative period I had studied law, and removed to Springfield to practice it. In 1846 I was once elected to the lower House of Congress. Was not a candidate for reelection. From 1849 to 1854, both inclusive, practiced law more assiduously than ever before. Always a Whig in politics; and generally on the Whig electoral tickets, making active canvasses. I was losing interest in politics when the repeal of the Missouri compromise aroused me again. What I have done since then is pretty well known.

If any personal description of me is thought desirable, it may be said I am, in height, 6 feet, 4 inches, nearly; lean in flesh, weighing on an average one hundred and eighty pounds; dark complexion, with coarse black hair and gray eyes. No other marks or brands recollected.[81]

Chapter 6

Setting the Political Stage

In the late 1850s the power of the political parties provided the political glue for cohesion in government. By that time there were two major parties—Republican and Democrat. The Democratic Party was a national party with an organization in all states. James Buchanan, the president, was a Democrat. The Republican Party was the new kid on the block. In 1860, it would make its second run for the White House and its roots were solely in the North.

The primary founding premise of the Republican Party was its stand on the slavery issue. Lincoln and his friends were there at its formation in Illinois. It was a sectional party in 1856, when it first entered presidential politics, with no party history, party pride, or party idols. Although Republicans would fight each other bitterly on other issues, they shared a common goal: preventing the extension of slavery.

The Republicans' first candidate for president, John C. Fremont, was defeated, winning all free states except Illinois, Indiana, New Jersey, Pennsylvania, and California. In 1860, a Republican victory needed only the addition of three of the four states of the lower North—Illinois, Indiana, New Jersey, and Pennsylvania—to the Republican list of states won by Fremont in 1856.

When the party lost the 1856 election, a vacuum was created at the top, waiting to be filled. There was no good-old-boy network in the Republican Party at that time and no person wore the mantle of Mr. Republican. However, many wanted desperately to fill the void, especially the party's leader in the Senate, William H. Seward of New York. Seward considered himself the teacher of Republican doctrines.[82]

In addition to Seward, a number of other names were being bandied about as presidential timber. They were, to name the more prominent, Senator Salmon Chase of Ohio; Senator Simon Cameron, the political boss of Pennsylvania; Judge Edward Bates of Missouri; Senator William Dayton of New Jersey; and Judge John McLean, associate justice of the Supreme Court.

In mid-December 1859, Lincoln received a Christmas gift that boosted his presidential chances considerably, courtesy of Norman Judd, the former anti-Nebraska Democrat who had tenaciously supported Lyman Trumbull and voted against Lincoln for United States Senator in 1855. Judd, now chairman of the Illinois Republican State Central Committee and the Illinois member on the Republican National Committee, journeyed to New York in mid-December 1859 to attend a meeting at the Astor House that would decide the site of the 1860 Republican Convention. Before Judd left for New York, Lincoln had written him a letter and reminded him that their friends believed it important the convention be held in Illinois.[83] His friends apparently realized that if the convention was held in any other state, Lincoln's chances for success dropped dramatically. Joseph Medill, editor and part owner of the *Chicago Tribune,* also attended the meeting, lobbying for Chicago as the convention site. Several other cities favored by one or another of the prospective candidates were under consideration and vying for the convention.

"Friends of Seward argued that the convention should meet in some New York city; Chase men were sure Cleveland or Columbus would be the ideal location. Bates men told how the Party would actually carry Missouri if the convention would only meet in St. Louis."[84] Indianapolis was turned down because it lacked sufficient hotel accommodations. While Bates's supporters wanted St. Louis, that city was turned down because Missouri, as a slave state, was certain to be carried by the Democrats in the next election. Sharply alert but seemingly casual, Judd, with tongue in cheek, suggested

William H. Seward

a compromise and pulled off a "manoeuvre [sic] of importance."[85] Assuring the committee that Chicago could take care of large crowds, he claimed that since Illinois had no prominent presidential candidate, Chicago would be a neutral site for a contest among Seward, Chase, and Bates. Quite possibly there were no serious objections raised because the other committee members considered a challenge from Lincoln remote at best.[86] The committee, with Judd voting, decided on Chicago by a single vote.[87] To win the nomination, all contenders had to come to Illinois and beat Lincoln on his own turf.

Suddenly, Lincoln's presidential glimmer went from the subjective "I wish" to the objective "I can." He had to start making definite plans on how to capture his dream. Lincoln realized he had to leap numerous hurdles during the next six months. He also realized that failure to clear any hurdle that appeared would, in all likelihood, sink his chances.

With Chicago the convention site, Lincoln had the home field advantage, a definite plus for the unannounced Lincoln campaign. Conversely, if the convention had been held in any other city the odds for his chances for the nomination would have dropped dramatically and, in all likelihood, been fatal to his candidacy.

Chicago, at that time, was a bustling city of more than 100,000 souls, most of them Republican and determined to help a hometown boy make good. Home field advantage meant the newspapers, the crowds, and the publicity would be heavily in favor of Lincoln and, more important, home field advantage meant that all rivals would be outsiders in Chicago.

As the election year dawned, Lincoln was still a noncandidate. In late January 1860, he met with some lawyer friends in an exploratory session in Springfield, Illinois. At their insistence, and believing the time was favorable, he gave them permission to advance his cause but not launch his candidacy.[88] It marked Lincoln's first overt steps to set his campaign in motion. Other than writing to Judd about the importance of having the national convention in Illinois, this was probably the first time he permitted himself to say openly that he would seek the nomination.

On February 11, 1860, a Lincoln biography appeared in the *Chester County Times* in Pennsylvania, courtesy of Jesse Fell. Fell had sent Lincoln's short biography to Joseph J. Lewis, of Westchester, Pennsylvania. Lewis prepared and sent to other Pennsylvania newspapers a sketch under the heading "Who is Abraham Lincoln?" In about 3,000 words, Lewis introduced Lincoln to Pennsylvanians. The sketch explained and put a favorable spin on "how so great and popular a man as Lincoln had twice been defeated for the Senate in his own State. . . . He had been defeated in 1854 through his own magnanimity and his unwillingness to permit the possible election of a proslavery man; and he was defeated in 1858 through the operation of 'an old and grossly unequal apportionment of the districts.'"[89]

Cooper Union

Chapter 7

Taking on the East

The previous October Lincoln had received and accepted an invitation to make a speech in February 1860 in New York at Henry Ward Beecher's Plymouth Church in Brooklyn.[90] He jumped at the chance to show he could identify with the voters in the East. It was mutually agreed the speech could be of a political nature.[91] The sponsors of the speech were opponents of Senator William Seward.[92] They had extended speaking invitations to prominent politicians (Francis P. Blair, Jr., was the first, Cassius Clay, the second, and Lincoln the third) in hopes of finding one who could excite the people and challenge Seward.[93] When Lincoln arrived in New York, he found out sponsorship had been taken over by the Young Men's Central Republican Union and that he would speak instead at the Cooper Institute in Manhattan on February 27, 1860.[94]

He was well aware the success of his speech would be judged on the ideas he espoused, the emotions he could arouse, and on his ability to communicate his enthusiasm to the people of New York City. If his reading of the Republican mood was correct—which the public reaction to his previous speeches led him to believe was accurate—and if his position on the slavery question was in harmony with mainstream Republicans, he was confident he could excite the people and show them he was up to the task of contending with any and all rivals for the nomination.

For his topic and subject matter Lincoln again looked to his long-time political antagonist, Senator Stephen A. Douglas, for motivation and inspiration. Douglas had published an article in the September 1859 issue of *Harper's New Monthly Magazine* wherein he again made the pitch for popular sovereignty, and hoped his article would reestablish his support in the South.[95]

Douglas claimed the founding fathers left it to the states and territories to decide the slavery question. Lincoln set about preparing his reply and, according to his law partner William Herndon, spent more time researching it than any other in his career, spending hours investigating what the founding fathers thought and did about slavery, reading Elliot's *Debates on the Federal Constitution,* a six-volume study, and perusing the *Congressional Globe.*[96]

Lincoln "realized that his destiny hung, to a large extent, on his Cooper Union Speech. On the impression he made in New York the East would judge his soundness as presidential timber."[97] He painstakingly researched and wrote the speech. On his way to New York City, he stopped off in Chicago to confer with two of his most ardent supporters, Dr. Charles Ray and Joseph Medill, owners of the *Chicago Tribune.* He asked them to review and critique what he had written. Later, when these gentlemen read the verbatim account of the speech they noted that Lincoln did not implement a single suggestion. "'Well,' said Ray sourly after reading it, 'he must have thrown our suggestions out of the train window!'"[98]

But, for a number of reasons, Lincoln was confident he could excite the crowd and felt his introduction to the "better, but busier citizens of New York"[99] would be successful. He was probably one of the best, if not the best, stump speakers in America in 1860, a communicator par excellence. His oratory always stirred the spirits and excited the people. His debates with Douglas and his speeches in Indiana and Ohio, all before thousands of spectators, justified his optimism.

Second, and probably most important, the Cooper Union speech would not be his first speech on the slavery issue. Lincoln had spoken out about slavery ever since he came out of political hibernation. He had refined, honed and perfected his message through numerous repetitions. He had learned what worked with audiences and what didn't work. He had also learned how to pace his speeches and connect with his audiences.

Finally, Lincoln realized the Cooper Union address would probably be his most important speech ever and, because of its importance to his political future, he crafted a speech that would command the attention of his sophisticated Eastern audience. More important, the speech was to be "an exceedingly clear and able presentation of the origin, principles, history, and purposes of the Republican Party. . . ."[100]

In *Lincoln for the Ages*, Johnson E. Fairchild described Lincoln's assignation with destiny:

> On Monday the twenty-seventh the Young Republican committee on arrangements called at the Astor House. Although it was raining they took Lincoln for a ride up Broadway to Mathew B. Brady's studio, where he faced the great photographer's camera for the first time. Apparently they were upset by the unprepossessing appearance of Mr. Lincoln, his bluff, awkward gestures, and his ignorance of the superficial manners and customs of the metropolitan sophisticates. Later on in the day the rain turned to snow, a poor omen for a large crowd. However, this was election year and the tall, gaunt, beardless, 51-year-old Illinois lawyer was a potential candidate and he was known to oppose slavery. As a result at least fifteen hundred people, described by the press as "the pick and flower of New York" and "a large and brilliant" group gathered. . . .

> Lincoln's great height and his ill-fitting new suit made him look somewhat peculiar and unusual. His jacket was too small, the sleeves were much too short. His trousers, perhaps wet from the snow or rain, were unpressed, and he seemed to limp or stagger a little. His new shoes hurt his feet.

> Lincoln started slowly; in fact he almost lost his audience in the first few sentences. He apparently suffered from stage fright or nervousness at the grandeur and size of the Great Hall and at the importance of the people he was to address. The platform guests alone could help a man a long way toward the Presidency. To top it all, his attack—his first words—failed. His voice cracked into a high falsetto and he referred to William Cullen Bryant as "Mr. Cheerman." Derisive comments were made and the people yelled, "Louder!" Many people shook their heads in disappointment, others

laughed. The crowd rustle increased. It was a bad opening, but as Lincoln warmed to his speech his voice lowered a little. His Springfield friend Mason Brayman sat at the back of the hall. By arrangement with Lincoln he was to raise his high hat on a cane whenever Lincoln did not speak loudly enough. Joseph R. Choate, the lawyer and diplomat, wrote of Lincoln at Cooper Union that "as he spoke he was transformed; his eyes kindled, his voice rang and his face shone and seemed to light up the whole assembly. For an hour and a half he held the audience in the hollow of his hand."[101]

Lincoln's research had exposed the speciousness of Douglas's claims and, in developing his speech, Lincoln used his uncanny ability to draw on the past to assess the present. He first explored the roots of the sectional strife between North and South. He then pressed the view that our forefathers believed Congress could control slavery in the territories. To support his conclusion, Lincoln examined the views of 39 signers of the Constitution and noted that 21 of the 39 believed that Congress could control slavery in the territories and not allow it to expand.[102] This view, he argued, was directly in sync with the Republican stance; it was the Republicans who were conservative and not, as claimed by the Democrats, revolutionary. He said the Republican Party was only following the principles set out by "our fathers, who framed the Government under which we live." Lincoln, in 11 words, pointed out the fallacy of the principle of Douglas's popular sovereignty concept: "if one man would enslave another, no third man should object."[103]

He took aim at the South's insistence it had the constitutional right to take slaves into the federal territories and to hold them there as property. He argued that the right of property in a slave is not distinctly and expressly affirmed in the Constitution.[104] He pointed out that the institution of slavery is not directly mentioned in the Constitution using the words "slavery" or "Negro race," but only by implication.

Lincoln's Cooper Union speech covered two more issues. He addressed the South's accusation that Republicans stirred up insurrections among their slaves, referring to John Brown's failed raid on Harper's Ferry in October 1859 aimed at acquiring arms for his effort to liberate slaves. He asserted that John Brown was not a Republican and no Republican was involved in the Harper's Ferry enterprise.[105] Said Lincoln, "John Brown's effort was peculiar. It was not a slave insurrection. It was an attempt by white men to get up a revolt among slaves, in which the slaves refused to participate."[106]

He responded to the South's declaration that the election of a Republican president would cause it to secede from the Union and that the dissolution would be the fault of the North: "That is cool. A highwayman holds a pistol to my ear, and mutters through his teeth, 'Stand and deliver, or I shall kill you and then you will be a murderer.'"[107]

He closed his speech by making his audience aware of their obligations as Republicans, urging his listeners to "HAVE FAITH, LET US, TO THE END, DARE TO DO OUR DUTY AS WE UNDERSTAND IT."[108] Although many had entered the hall in doubt as to their duty, they "went away with their path bright before them."[109]

Lincoln wanted to captivate his audience with the depth of his understanding of the slavery question and to set the party's ideological stand on that issue. He surpassed his expectations. It was, without a doubt, a political *tour de force* and many Lincoln biographers claim it was the speech that "boosted Lincoln's reputation so vigorously that he became Seward's leading competitor for the presidential nomination."[110] He had stirred the fount of imagination of the Republican faithful.

So mesmerizing was his performance, Noah Brooks of the *New York Tribune* reported, that one listener proclaimed, "He's the greatest man since St. Paul."[111] Lincoln's evaluation of his speech, however, was not quite as lofty. He wrote his wife Mary that the Cooper Union speech, "being within my calculation before I started, went off passably well, and gave me no trouble whatever."[112]

No sooner had Lincoln finished speaking than Horace Greeley, publisher of the *New York Tribune,* sensing a new political star had risen in the West, approached him and, wanting to print the speech in its entirety for his readers, asked him "to read the proofs of his speech."[113] Lincoln, surprised and flattered, readily consented and later that night he visited the office of the *Tribune* and proofread the copy.[114]

The following editorial appeared in the February 28, 1860, issue of the *Tribune:*

> The Speech of Abraham Lincoln at the Cooper Institute last evening was one of the happiest and most convincing political arguments ever made in this City, and was addressed to a crowded and most appreciating audience. Since the days of Clay and Webster no man has spoken to a larger assemblage of the intellect and mental culture of our City. *Mr. Lincoln is one of Nature's orators,* using his rare powers solely and effectively to elucidate and to convince, though their inevitable effect is to delight and electrify as well. We present herewith a very full and accurate report of this speech; yet the tones, the gestures, the kindling eye and the mirth-provoking look, defy the reporter's skill. The vast assemblage frequently rang with cheers and shouts of applause, which were prolonged and intensified at the close. *No man ever before made such an impression on his first appeal to a New York audience. . . .* [115] [Emphasis added.]

Overnight Success

Success begets success and, seizing upon the opportunity to further his unannounced candidacy and pan for additional political nuggets, he quickly followed up his Cooper Union speech with a whirlwind tour of the Northeast. Word rapidly spread of the power of his oratory. Overnight he had become the attraction of the Northeast. Party leaders invited him to speak in Connecticut, Rhode Island, and New Hampshire, where state elections would soon be held.

Although the primary reason for his trip to the Northeast was to visit his son Robert at Phillips Exeter Academy in New Hampshire, Lincoln managed to speak in 11 cities in 12 days. His speeches in New England were devoted almost entirely to the slavery issue, delivered before large audiences, and made newspaper headlines all over the North. Lincoln was making news rather than following news.

The speeches also fostered his political persona as an available candidate for the presidency. He had, through his debates with Douglas and his many speeches throughout the North, defined and justified the accepted Republican position on slavery. In fact, ever since he committed to the Republican Party in 1856, he had become the Republicans' most clear and eloquent voice on the slavery issue.

Lincoln's swing through New England demonstrated that he could generate a genuine magic in the spirits of the men who vote. The crowds loved him. At each stop, the outpouring of goodwill toward him was staggering. "His tour became a triumph as Republican admirers thronged his train to accompany him from one town to another,"[116] and Lincoln learned the people of the Northeast judged a man "by what he is, and what he can do, and not by the cloth he wears, the knowledge he has acquired, the wealth he possesses, or the blood that flows in his veins."[117]

He knew who the local power players were and, during his tour, he cultivated their friendship and sought their views. In particular, Lincoln knew how to romance the newspaper media. Herndon put it more aptly, "In common with other politicians he never overlooked a newspaper man who had it in his power to say a good or bad thing of him."[118]

While in Hartford, Lincoln visited with newspaperman Gideon Welles for an hour. Welles, deeply impressed by Lincoln's "clear as crystal" logic, later wrote a "good thing" about him in an editorial.[119] Welles would go to the Chicago convention as a delegate from Connecticut.

The party leaders in Connecticut, New Hampshire, and Rhode Island loved him; he excited them. Lincoln was treated royally and, for his candidacy, the timing of his success could not have been better. The Republican convention was less than three months away.

When his one-man show concluded its Eastern run, Lincoln returned home a dominant political force, increasingly optimistic about his chances for capturing the presidential nomination. "When he went East he had had some thought of the Vice Presidency but the success of his Cooper Union speech made him a candidate for President."[120] "His recent success had stimulated his self-confidence to unwonted proportions,"[121] and Lincoln was inching closer to

Gideon Welles

becoming an avowed candidate for the Republican presidential nomination. A little later, when a political friend asked if he was a candidate,[122] he conceded that "the taste is in my mouth a little."[123]

Shortly after he arrived back home, Lincoln began receiving letters from newfound friends about his efforts in the Northeast and his chances for the nomination. He learned because of the closeness of the recent elections in Connecticut his name was "mentioned more freely than ever" for the nomination "by some who have had other views, or whose feelings were previously committed in favor of another [namely Senator William H. Seward]."[124] They feared defeat if Seward was the nominee. A Minnesota man wrote that in order for the Republicans to win, the ticket should read "Lincon [sic] and some good republican [sic]" rather than "some good Republican and Lincon [sic]."[125] An Ohio supporter advised that the nominee of the party could not be an extreme man but must be moderate in political views and that Lincoln filled the bill.[126] A Kansas supporter correctly described Lincoln's political position as a compromise candidate. He viewed the Republican party with a "head" (Seward), a "tail" (Bates), and a "middle" (Lincoln). If the convention selects the head, the tail will drop off, and if it selects the tail, the head will drop off; however, if nominated, Lincoln "could hold the head and tail on and beat the Democracy."[127]

Finally, an Illinois supporter expressed not only delight in the success of Lincoln's tour in the East but closed with the announcement that there was "a little Abraham Lincoln at our house, about 24 hours old—His arrival created something of a Stir in our little town as it got noised around that your Honor was at Mr. Hays, and Several persons were on their way to call on you, when it was discovered that it was not the original, but only a namesake."[128]

Stoking the Home Fires

Although Lincoln was greatly encouraged by his correspondence from admirers and supporters, he first had to oversee a little political housekeeping at home. Before moving on to Chicago to capture the nomination, he had to mobilize his support in Illinois.

Over the last year Lincoln had taken great pains to control the intra-party bickering. He had had to act forcefully and yet impartially in the balancing of the competing ambitions of his friends. Three of his friends—Norman Judd, Leonard Swett, and Richard Yates—were seeking the gubernatorial nomination and, because these three men were members of the party's hierarchy and he needed their combined support, Lincoln advised them he would take no part whatsoever in their campaigns.[129]

When the party bickering escalated into legal warfare and Norman Judd sued John Wentworth's paper for libel, Lincoln took an active role in restoring peace, and the matter, while not harmoniously resolved, was satisfactorily settled without splitting the party.[130] Lincoln had held the disparate groups together and, because of his peacekeeping efforts, he knew the party hierarchy was in his corner. Now it was time for the rank and file to climb on his bandwagon.

Lincoln had expressed concern to Norman Judd shortly before he had left for New York in February 1860 that while it would not hurt him to be nominated on the national ticket, it would hurt him not to get the endorsement of the Illinois delegates.[131] Lincoln knew Senator Seward had strength in northern Illinois and Judge Edward Bates had support in southern Illinois. He asked for Judd's help in Judd's part of the vineyard, which included Chicago.[132] A short time later the *Chicago Tribune* threw its support to Lincoln and endorsed him for president.[133]

Despite that endorsement, when the Illinois Republicans met in Decatur, his chances of success in winning the presidential sweepstakes of 1860 took a decided downturn. It would no longer be Lincoln against the world; now his success or failure was contingent on the actions and abilities of others. For him to achieve his dream, his friends had to deliver—or else.

One piece of luck for the Republicans in general was the Democrats' disarray. In April 1860, the Democrats held their nominating convention at Charleston, South Carolina. Senator

Stephen A. Douglas was the odds-on favorite, but his response to Lincoln's loaded question at the Freeport debate—that a territory could legally keep slavery out of a territory—came back to haunt him. The traditional rule that governs Democratic national conventions is that a candidate needs a two-thirds majority to win the nomination. (The Republicans at their 1860 national convention required only a simple majority for nomination.) This meant that for Douglas to be successful, he needed the support of the South. Instead, the Southern states put up a solid front against him. After 57 ballots with no candidate receiving the required two-thirds majority, the convention adjourned without a nomination. Although the Democratic Party was divided and in complete disarray, when it reconvened in June, Senator Douglas would probably head the Northern Democratic ticket, with Southern Democrats splitting off. A divided Democratic Party greatly increased the odds for a Republican victory in November.

The disintegration of the Democratic Party, while presaging a Republican victory, was threatening the stability of the Union. Congress had been in session five months and, of that time, nearly two months was spent in selecting the Speaker of the House. Confrontations on the House floor were becoming commonplace; threats of disunion "punctuated all the debates."[134] According to one newspaperman of the day, the Southern Democrats, still "in a white heat of passion over John Brown and Harpers Ferry, were fuller than ever of bluster and bravado, and the North had begun to send men to Congress who talked back and could not be bullied."[135]

Orville H. Browning

Chapter 8

The March Begins

The meeting of the Republican Party of Illinois in Decatur on May 9 and 10, 1860, a week before the Chicago convention, was the beginning of Lincoln's march to the nomination. The Illinois meeting was called to, among other things, nominate candidates for state offices, endorse a candidate for the presidency, and select delegates to the Chicago convention. The action taken at Decatur was an indispensable first step toward Lincoln's nomination. His friends began their preparations. One friend, Richard J. Oglesby, was in charge of the arrangements for the state convention. He was determined to stamp the upcoming Lincoln campaign with a common touch. He believed the campaign needed a marketable slogan, a catchy nickname that would not only project Lincoln as a candidate who could identify with the people, but also trigger a positive image.[136]

Oglesby was familiar with Lincoln's humble beginnings and his courageous fight against the spread of slavery, and he set out to learn about Lincoln's unknown qualities and develop some sort of connection to the common people. There was an old-timer living in Decatur—John Hanks, a Lincoln cousin. Hanks, Lincoln, and another man had ferried a shipment of goods—corn, pigs, and produce—from Springfield to New Orleans years before. For their labors, each man received $12 a month.[137]

In the days of their youth, the cousins "had split rails, toiled in cornfield and on flatboat together, sleeping and watching in snow and rain. Their lives were bound as with leather thongs."

Hanks had been a Democrat. He had voted for Douglas in 1858.[138] Oglesby was also a friend of Hanks and when he asked Hanks what Abe was good at, Hanks indicated while Abe was real good at "dreaming," they had split rails together 30 years ago. Intrigued, Oglesby wondered if any of the rails were still in existence and, a few days before the convention assembled, he and Hanks took a buggy ride out to the site of the first Lincoln family farm. After they traveled about 10 miles, they came to an old fence of locust and black walnut rails. Hanks declared them to be the very ones he and Abe had mauled many years ago. Oglesby retrieved two rails, dragged them to town under his buggy, hid them in his barn, and readied them for their debut as Lincoln campaign hype.[139]

"Before the Convention met," said Oglesby, "I talked with several Republicans about my plan, and we fixed it up that old John Hanks should take the rails into the Convention. We made a banner, attached to a board across the top of the rails with the inscription:

ABRAHAM LINCOLN
The Rail Candidate
For President in 1860
Two rails from a lot of 3,000 made in 1830 by
John Hanks and Abe Lincoln, whose father
was the first pioneer of Macon County."[140]

While Lincoln expected to be endorsed as the party's choice for president, he attended the Decatur convention, "but for a time he kept out of sight. He awaited the psychological moment for his appearance."[141] Shortly after the lunch break on the day it convened, the name of Abraham Lincoln was presented to the delegates as their choice for president. "The motion was seconded with enthusiasm, and was about to be put to a vote."[142] Oglesby, the presiding officer, called for Lincoln to have a seat on the platform and Lincoln was "seized and lifted over the spectators to the stand, amid loud applause."[143] Sensing the psychological moment to spring his theatrics had arrived, Oglesby announced that an old Macon County Democrat wished to make a presentation. The crowd again roared its approval and, on cue, John Hanks and a friend came marching through the crowd bearing two rails upright. The crowd loved it and, for 15 minutes, "cheered, screamed, tossed hats and newspapers high in the air and pommeled [sic] one another. . . ."[144]

When the demonstration subsided, Lincoln's reply caused it to erupt anew:

> Gentlemen, I suppose you want to know something about those things (pointing to old John and the rails). Well, the truth is, John Hanks and I did make rails in the Sangamon Bottom. I don't know whether we made these rails or not; the fact is, I don't think they are a credit to the makers (laughing as he spoke). But I do know this: I made rails then, and I think I could make better ones than these now.[145]

Oglesby's "spectacular coup"[146] had the desired effect. Not only was the motion passed unanimously, it was pure, unadulterated American politics at its creative best and demonstrated the extraordinary impact Lincoln had on the emotions of ordinary people. Above all, Oglesby's little drama had coined a compelling campaign slogan: "Abraham Lincoln, Rail-Splitter," a slogan that showed in a dramatic way Lincoln's connection to the common man, that his seed was from their seed, his stock from their stock. The nickname quickly caught on. A few days later, when his nomination for president was seconded by an Ohio delegate, Lincoln was referred to as "the man who can split rails and maul Democrats."[147]

Oglesby finished the story:

> From that time forward the rail was ever present in the campaign. There was a great demand for Lincoln rails. John Hanks sold the two that he brought into the Convention. A man from Kentucky gave him five dollars for one. The next day he went out and got a wagonload, and put them in my barn. He sold them for a dollar apiece. Then other people went into the business, and the supply seemed inexhaustible.[148]

The town of Decatur held a certain significance in the life of Abraham Lincoln as the scene of two of the most poignant events in his life. He nostalgically remembered the town as a place of beginning. In the spring of 1856, he had stood in front of the courthouse in Decatur and "looked across the Public Square. The area was not and is not large. Lincoln was mentally measuring the square and endeavoring to locate a particular spot. Presently he walked a little distance into the square, and said to his companion, Henry C. Whitney, 'Here is the exact spot where I stood by our wagon when we moved from Indiana 26 years ago; this isn't six feet from the exact spot.'"[149] Lincoln had come to Decatur a "poor, uneducated and unknown boy" and now 30 years later, because of the action taken at Decatur, his name would be presented at the Republican National Convention as a candidate for president of the United States.[150]

The convention named a committee to select the Chicago delegates. That evening the delegate committee "walked with Lincoln out to a quiet place on a railroad tract where they sat down and talked."[151] The selection of delegates was not a cut-and-dried affair. Because Seward had support in northern Illinois and Bates support in southern Illinois, Lincoln and his friends, wanting to maximize his control over the delegation, had to develop a plan to unify the Illinois delegation.

Lincoln had to make some hard choices, especially in the selection of the at-large delegates. He wanted to choose men who represented the various segments of the party. Two choices were particularly troublesome. First, Orville Browning, who had tried cases associated with Lincoln and had spent evenings at the Lincoln home in Springfield, was a powerful Republican who favored Edward Bates for the nomination. Lincoln was aware of his preference, and on February 8, 1860, he had visited with Browning and they "had a free talk about the Presidency." Browning noted in his diary that Lincoln thought Browning "may be right in supposing Mr. Bates to be the strongest and best man we can run—that he can get votes even in this County he [Lincoln] cannot get—and that there is a large class of voters in all the free States that would go for Mr. Bates, and for no other man."[152] Because of Browning's preference, Richard Oglesby was in favor of deleting Browning from the list of delegates to the Chicago National Convention.[153] Lincoln's dilemma: if Browning was not selected as a delegate, it could make an enemy of him and there was the possibility he would go to the convention and create mischief.[154] Lincoln decided it was more prudent to select him and his decision paid him many dividends.

Second was whether to name John Wentworth, Chicago's mayor and editor of the *Chicago Democrat,* as a delegate. Some viewed Wentworth as a loose cannon and described him, one author wrote, as the Illinois Machiavelli.[155] One of Lincoln's friends, Judge David Davis, was of the opinion Wentworth was indeed a Lincoln supporter. Davis had written Lincoln that he would vouch for Wentworth's faithfulness.[156] However, Wentworth and Lincoln supporter Norman A. Judd hated one another and were bitter political enemies. Their feud had escalated into open warfare when Judd sued Wentworth's *Democrat* for libel. Apparently Judd was persuasive. Wentworth was not selected as a delegate. Of course, Wentworth returned to Chicago bent on revenge and determined to do whatever he could to create problems for Lincoln.[157]

On May 10, 1860, as soon as the delegates to the Republican Convention were selected, John Palmer introduced a resolution that "Abraham Lincoln is the choice of the Republican party of Illinois for the Presidency, and the delegates from this State are instructed to use all honorable means to secure his nomination by the Chicago Convention, and to vote as a unit for him."[158] This was the same John Palmer who, as one of the five anti-Nebraska Democrats, supported Trumbull's senatorial race against Lincoln in 1855.

When a pro-Seward delegate made some remarks against the resolution, Palmer delivered a powerful rebuttal speech and all opposition was quickly beaten down. The resolution passed unanimously. The Illinois Republicans endorsed Lincoln's candidacy and went to the convention as Lincoln team players, even those who were privately for other candidates. Now these 22 delegates "would make a hard sustained fight for Lincoln instead of voting briefly for him and then going over to another man."[159]

John Wentworth

Abraham Lincoln, in uncontested control of the Illinois Republican Party, could not have asked for more. His old friends and his new friends came through brilliantly. When the Decatur meeting adjourned, Lincoln was, at the very least, a favorite-son player in the presidential sweepstakes of 1860. If Lincoln had any reservations about the abilities of his friends to wage a national campaign, the events at Decatur removed all doubts.

Candidates in 1860 did not attend national conventions. They stayed away, above the fray. Lincoln and the other possible nominees went home and anxiously waited for the telegraph to click its news from Chicago. Seward went to his home in Auburn, Bates to his estate outside St. Louis, Chase to Cincinnati, and, reluctantly, Lincoln returned to Springfield, "careful that no public statements should come from him [during this time],"[160] and paced the sidelines. His political fate was in the hands of his friends, completely out of his control.

David Davis

Chapter 9

Davis Heads the Campaign

L incoln selected Judge David Davis as his campaign manager in Chicago. Davis was the presiding judge of the Eighth Circuit, a judicial circuit comprising 14 counties. During the 10-plus years Lincoln actively practiced and traveled the circuit, a special relationship had developed, not only between the two men but among all riders on the circuit.[161] Six months of every year, for 10 years, they (Lincoln, the judge, and the other lawyers) lived together on the circuit. Not only did they look one another in the eye in the courtroom, they rode from county seat to county seat together, shared the same accommodations, ate their meals together, and after court adjourned, sometimes "far into the night they talked, argued, joked, and told stories." They looked upon themselves as members of a close-knit fraternity, possibly closer than family.

Because of this bond, Davis was a Lincoln loyalist to his core. Lincoln's opponents would soon find out that Davis was willing to work without sleep and was a good organizer and a behind-the-scenes dynamo more than ready to do battle for his candidate. Davis was in complete control. He would organize and direct all activities of the Lincoln task force.

Davis firmly believed Lincoln had an aura of distinction, that he was head and shoulders above the pack, and the judge was bound and determined to secure the nomination for his friend. When Lincoln had lost the Senate race to Douglas in 1858, Davis consoled Lincoln, regretting he had not resigned his judgeship to help in the senatorial campaign.[162] He was determined to make amends and would have the opportunity to do so during the fight for the 1860 Republican presidential nomination.

Judge Davis was a large man, weighing more than 300 pounds. Once on the circuit he admonished a lawyer who had a drinking problem and was seeking his third continuance on a particular case, "I must give you some advice. You must drink less and work more, or you will roll in the gutter."

Taking umbrage, the lawyer responded, "And I must give your Honor some advice. You must eat less and eliminate more or you will bust."[163] What makes the verbal exchange even sweeter is that once when the judge attended a temperance meeting, the same attorney had been the featured speaker.[164]

Davis's train arrived in Chicago on Saturday, May 12. Abraham Lincoln's presidential aspirations rested squarely on his large shoulders. He was accompanied on the trip by three of his lieutenants, all associates of Lincoln in law and politics—Stephen A. Logan, Leonard Swett, and Jesse Dubois. For the next week the dedicated amateurs would have very little rest. Leonard Swett later wrote that during the week he did not sleep two hours a night.[165]

As the train meandered to Chicago, the Lincoln team had a sense they were probably making history. To them Lincoln had outgrown his favorite-son status and had become a threatening dark horse. They were optimistic that the campaign was gathering momentum daily and the best was yet to come.

There was ample reason for optimism. The Illinois newspapers were behind Lincoln, the Illinois Republican Party hierarchy was behind him, and the rank and file had closed ranks behind him. Add to this Judd's coup in securing the convention for Chicago and all boded well for Lincoln's candidacy.

Lincoln's selection of Davis as his campaign manager was a masterstroke of political know-how. Although Davis had never before headed a national campaign, he had natural political instincts and an innate sense of how decisions are made at political conventions. He was a shrewd, practical politician. He realized that practical politics, and not speeches, win nominations. For all the prestige and notoriety the brilliant speeches of Lincoln won in his debates with Douglas and at Cooper Union and then the Northeast— Lincoln was dubbed by Horace Greeley as one of nature's orators— it would not change the vote of a single delegate to the Chicago convention.[166] Convention politics in 1860 was shaped by behind-the-scene political machinations "in innumerable caucuses in animated hotel rooms alive with politicians, money, smoke, liquor, gossip."[167]

The Lincoln team was a new organization, operating on the national stage for the first time. However, they were daring enough to believe they had a legitimate chance for the nomination and smart enough to figure out how to do it. Davis knew it was up to him and his team to harness and put to good use the bursting energies of the Illinois base, to mobilize and direct scores of Lincoln enthusiasts and supporters during the next seven days. Knowing the political realities, Davis and his team were ready to storm the trenches to do battle with all foes. Their sole mission and goal was to have Abraham Lincoln nominated. The challenge facing them was how to defeat better-known and more experienced rivals for the presidential nomination.

Davis knew the book on all the presidential candidates and, as a good campaign manager, he knew the major opposition at the convention would come from three players: Senator William H. Seward, Senator Salmon Chase, and Judge Edward Bates. Of the remaining hopefuls, including Supreme Court Justice John McLean and Senator Simon Cameron of Pennsylvania, Cameron was the strongest, but only because Pennsylvania had the second largest delegate count of 54.

There were no doubts that Seward, on paper, was the most qualified candidate for the presidency. He, like Lincoln, a former Whig, was the leader of the Republicans; his political pedigree was second to none. He had executive experience and was practiced in international affairs. Seward had served as governor of New York for two terms. He was in his second term in the U.S. Senate. Among party insiders, it was conceded that he could have had the 1856 nomination over John C. Fremont, but Seward and his political partner and chief supporter, Thurlow Weed, determined that while Seward's chances would have been good in 1856, he would be a shoo-in in 1860.[168]

As the delegates were descending on Chicago, Seward was the acknowledged front-runner for the nomination. He had obtained commitments from a number of states. Straw votes taken on inbound trains confirmed his popularity:[169]

> One such ballot on a Michigan Central train of 12 coaches gave Seward 210 votes to 30 for all other candidates; on a Chicago & Northwestern train, Seward had 127 and all others, 44; on a Chicago & Rock Island train of 10 coaches, Seward again led with 113 to 41 for all others.[170]

Seward's faithful followers believed the Republican Party would collapse if Seward was not nominated: "Without him it would be a play without Hamlet."[171]

Seward's Vulnerability

But he had chinks in his political persona, a vulnerability that stemmed from his own behavior and his political association with Thurlow Weed. Many of the party faithful viewed Seward as a radical, primarily for two speeches. The first, a speech made in 1850 when he opposed the Compromise of 1850, set out his "doctrine of higher law." He proclaimed:

> It is true, indeed, that the national domain is ours. It is true that it was acquired by the valor and with the wealth of the whole nation. But we hold, nevertheless, no arbitrary power over anything, whether acquired lawfully or seized by usurpation. The Constitution regulates our stewardship; the Constitution devotes the domain to union, to justice, to defense, to welfare, and to liberty. But *there is a higher law than the Constitution*, which regulates our authority over this domain, and devotes it to the same noble purposes.[172] [Emphasis added.]

There is no doubt the "senator had thrilled many antislave crusaders when he faced southern legalists with the outcry that there was a 'higher law,' even above the Constitution, to which moral men owed obedience. But with those same words he had also affrighted many moderates," according to a Greeley biographer.[173]

The second speech was made in Rochester, New York, in October 1858, shortly after Lincoln's "House Divided" speech. In this speech, Seward expounded on the conflicts of the two systems, bond (slave) labor and free labor. He predicted:

> Shall I tell you what this collision means? They who think that it is accidental, unnecessary, the work of interested or fanatical agitators, and therefore ephemeral, mistake the case altogether. It is an *irrepressible conflict* between opposing and enduring forces, and it means that the United States must and will, sooner or later, become either entirely a slave-holding nation or entirely a free-labor nation.[174] [Emphasis added.]

While the speech rallied the militant with a blast proclaiming an "irrepressible conflict" between the free states and slavery states, it also "served to embitter against him all those who read into it the threat of a Northern crusade against the South."[175]

Seward's long political association with Thurlow Weed also proved a political liability in 1860. Weed, editor of the *Albany Evening Journal,* had always declined office. It was speculated by his enemies that Weed sought other rewards for being the man behind the throne. During the last legislative session in New York, he had been involved in the passage of a number of bills in return for franchise fees from the beneficiaries of the legislation that would be used in funding partisan political activities. Consequently, a number of party leaders regarded the Seward candidacy with suspicion and feared corruption if he was elected.[176]

As the leader of the Republicans in the Senate, Seward was on the receiving end of the Southern reaction to John Brown's raid in Virginia. He was attacked and berated as a revolutionary who cared nothing for the Union.[177] "The manifesto of Gov. Seward at Rochester, anticipates the riot at Harper's Ferry as inevitably as night follows day," according to the partisan *U.S. Democratic Review.*[178]

Also, Seward had angered an important faction in the Republican Party. As governor of New York, he had supported measures beneficial to Irish immigrants and had alienated, and would be unacceptable to, the suspicious Know Nothings. In those states where the Know Nothings held the balance of power—Illinois, Indiana, New Jersey, and Pennsylvania—Seward's candidacy was viewed as a liability to the party.

Leaders were worried that the recent elections in Connecticut and Rhode Island demonstrated the Republicans needed to select a candidate who was not radical and who would appeal to conservatives. The Republican governor in Connecticut, who had wide appeal, was reelected by 541 votes and a Democrat won in Rhode Island over a Republican with radical leanings.[179]

Seward had given his campaign the luster of prestige abroad in 1859 when he took a European trip from May to December and was greeted by heads of government. It didn't hurt that while he was making the rounds of European capitals, there was little chance for him to make a political misstep or faux pas at home. When he returned in December 1859, Seward tried to change his image and toned down his rhetoric. He "receded from the high-water mark of his 'irrepressible conflict,'" and "[h]is words in Congress no longer echoed the higher law and no longer demanded the end of slavery."[180] Seward was going after the middle ground. Moderation was the word, but his new tack made the abolitionists unhappy.

Salmon Chase of Ohio was another contender for the nomination. Having served as a U.S. senator and governor of Ohio, Chase had been one of the nation's first leading statesmen to join the Republican Party. He was "a man of intellectual vigor, spotless character, and commanding physique."[181] However, he, too, was viewed as a radical and he could not even unite the Ohio delegation behind his candidacy. He was qualified to be president, but he had no grasp of convention politics. He held the naïve conviction that his ability alone would project him into the presidency. "Though burning with presidential ambitions, he had no party managers, no important editors, and no Congressional friends to push him forward,"[182] and did nothing more than write letters. Chase would not seek the office; instead, he believed the people would demand him as their candidate.

Salmon P. Chase

Edward Bates of Missouri was 66 years old at the time of the convention. He had been courted by Republican Party leaders as an alternative to Seward. Though he was not yet a Republican, he was from a slave state and he could pass the Republican litmus test on slavery and other issues as well. A former slave owner, Bates was against slavery, "clinging to the doctrines of the revolutionary sages that 'slavery was an evil to be restricted, not a good to be diffused'" and opposed its extension. He was in favor of not only the immediate admission of Kansas into the Union, but an East-West railroad, and the passage of homestead legislation. His primary supporter was Horace Greeley, publisher of the *New York Tribune,* who wanted the Republican Party to expand out of the North and lose its sectional party tag. Greeley believed Bates, who was once a Whig, was essentially a Republican and would pull votes in the slave states and could rally Whig support behind him.[183]

Bates's supporters believed, with him heading the ticket, the party would, in all likelihood, win Missouri and have a good chance to win Tennessee and Maryland.[184] His nomination scenario required a deadlock in the convention and the Seward backers, once they knew Seward could not win, going outside the party to get a candidate.

The Bates supporters were telling their man that even though he was not a Republican, he was the best man to beat the Democrats. He believed what he was told. He became convinced his nomination was more probable than that of any other man. However, like Seward, he had a weakness. Bates was a former Know-Nothing and it was feared he would be a loser in those states where the foreign vote was critical to success.[185]

Simon Cameron was the political boss of Pennsylvania. He was a true entrepreneur—a newspaper publisher, financier, and builder of canals and railroads—who "amassed a personal fortune in public office, some said by unsavory means."[186] He had been elected to the U.S. Senate in 1857. Davis doubted if Cameron had any appeal outside of his home state. Cameron is, incidentally, credited with coining the phrase that "an honest politician is one who when bought stays bought."[187]

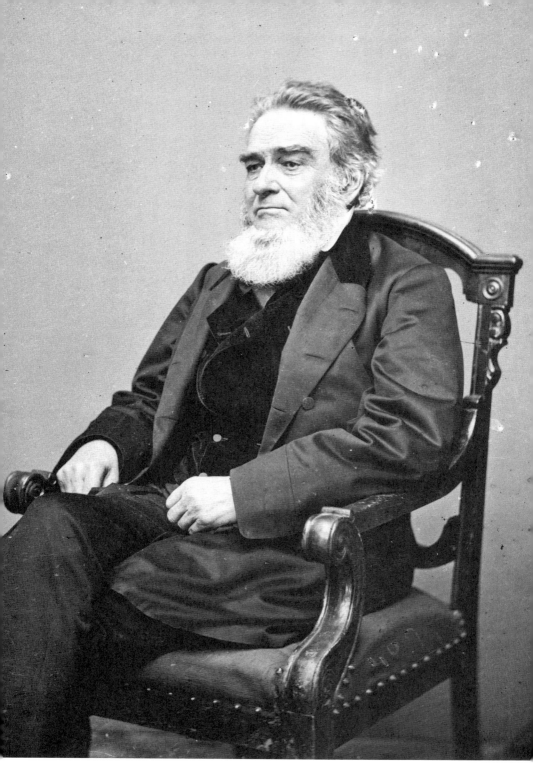

Edward Bates

Simon Cameron

John McLean

John McLean was 75 years old in 1860 and his limited political fame was for his dissenting opinion in the *Dred Scott* case. Davis reported to Lincoln a view that running McLean is like "running a dead man."[188]

These men had one thing in common. They were "great men, all of them, and they owed their reputation to their own achievements, and not to an accident of temporary elevation by opposition to a man of distinction, such as Senator Stephen Douglas."[189] However, although more conspicuous than Lincoln, "all had inveterate enemies."[190]

As Lincoln's campaign manager, Davis was aware that, in seeking the Republican nomination, his candidate was less prepared to be president than any of his rivals. The short autobiography Lincoln had prepared and sent to Jesse Fell disclosed Lincoln's shortcomings. He had no formal education and had an undistinguished political career. He had lost his last two elections, held no public office in 1860, had no executive experience whatsoever, and knew little of foreign affairs. On the other hand, Davis knew the times demanded a strong leader with charismatic qualities like Lincoln. Lincoln's strengths were that he had no public record to defend; his personal life was beyond reproach; he had no enemies within the party; he forged the Republican stand on slavery; and he was the one individual who could unite rather than divide all the contentious factions of the party. Better yet, he had already beaten the Democratic strongman—Senator Douglas—for the popular vote in the Senate campaign in 1858 and he could do it again.

Although just a faction within the Republican Party, the Know Nothings were a viable political force in the four critical states: Illinois, Indiana, New Jersey, and Pennsylvania. In the 1856 presidential election, the Know Nothing candidate, Millard Fillmore, received more than 21 percent of the total vote. "A slight shift of popular votes in Pennsylvania and Illinois would have thrown those states in the Republican column and elected Fremont."[191]

There were no doubts; Seward was the man to beat and Davis was confident he could be beaten.

Chapter 10

The Lincoln Team Gathers

During the third week in May 1860, Chicago was in "a tumult of expectation and preparation."[192] Delegations were coming from 19 free states, five slave states and three territories.[193] Chicago expected its population of 100,000 to swell by 40,000 during the week.

The political cauldron started to simmer as the party faithful began to gather the weekend before the convention opened. Starting on Saturday, the first of 465 delegates, newspaper representatives, party officials, and thousands of candidates' workers and supporters arrived and began preparations for the upcoming extravaganza. Because of Chicago's mushrooming growth, "more than four-fifths of its population having arrived within less than 10 years,"[194] the "immigrant Chicagoans organized as reception committees to receive in grand style the arriving delegation from their old home state."[195]

Chicago spared nothing to help stage a "monster show."[196] According to a Davis biographer:

> The city had dressed itself in gala attire. Billowing banners were suspended across the thoroughfares. Store and house fronts were draped with flags. Omnibuses were bandaged with bunting. Crowds in holiday mood marched through the muddy streets, cheering, waving to friends on the wooden sidewalks, and flaunting standards inscribed with the names of their favorite candidate—Chase, Cameron, Seward, or Lincoln. Explosions from miniature cannon and sputtering rockets called attention to unusual displays.[197]

Without doubt, the 1860 Republican Convention left a unique mark on the American political landscape. From 1860 on, the political convention would forever be a rugged, all-American political jousting tournament with a panache all its own—parades, banners, emblems, songs, speeches, and, most of all, noise.[198]

Delegate-hunting season had officially opened and all campaign managers "were exerting themselves frenziedly to convert the wavering, to intimidate the fearful, to bargain with the purchasable, and to outmaneuver, outbluff, and outswap their opponents."[199]

Nearly all delegates arrived by train and, inasmuch as this was only the second Republican national convention, most were strangers to one another. The delegates arrived on one of the 15 railroads serving Chicago, probably at an affordable, reduced fare. The delegates had a choice of accommodations available to fit every budget. There were seven first-class hotels for the big spenders, such as the Tremont House, the Richmond, the Briggs, and the sleek new Sherman, all charging $2.50 a night for their accommodations. For the leaner budget, there were 50 more hotels at $1.50 a night and 100 hotels at $1.[200] For those who wanted simpler arrangements, a rooming house stay cost even less.

As soon as the delegates, all men, unpacked their bags, they drifted over to visit the headquarters and hospitality suites of the various candidates. While indulging in the pleasures of a drink and a smoke, they engaged in convention shoptalk. The hotels were soon crowded to overflowing. Movement from room to room, if any could be observed, would be measured in inches rather than yards. The smell of politics permeated the air. Rumors circulated and recirculated until they had the ring of truth. While there "are a thousand rumors afloat and things of incalculable moment are communicated to you confidentially, at intervals of five minutes," said a reporter, "the probability is not one is possessed of a single political fact not known to the whole, which is of the slightest consequence to any human being."[201] Regardless, this was the time candidates jockeyed for position and engaged in preconvention horse-trading to insure their success.

The delegates were concerned citizens and took their responsibility seriously. There was a sense that life in America would be transformed by their choice for president, that their decision would have a direct effect on many lives not only in the country but on people all over the world. To a delegate they realized the presidential election of 1860 was within their grasp and the "nearness of it made everybody uncommonly fearful of losing it."[202] To win the White House and stop the extension of slavery, all they needed was a man who could carry the North.

As soon as their train reached the Chicago terminal, Davis and his crew hit the ground running. They would soon experience firsthand the awesome and unpredictable—yet exhilarating—war of convention politics. Davis assumed the role of a tactical general commanding a group of Lincoln loyalists against a group of outsiders who ventured into their homeland. Their days were ones of supreme exertion, as, without pause, the Lincoln team went from delegation to delegation trying to harvest the support that Lincoln's reputation had created. The nomination was no longer a remote possibility. With a run of luck and dogged determination, they could win it all.

When Davis arrived he found that all candidates, except Lincoln, had established headquarters in the hotels. He immediately corrected this oversight and rented two rooms at the Tremont House.[203] Now Lincoln had a headquarters, and from there the Lincoln team worked their political magic. Included in the inner circle were "almost all the influential friends Lincoln had in the State,"[204] including "all of Lincoln's old lawyer intimates."[205]

Support from the Heart

The men who formed the nucleus of his campaign team had a determination to win the nomination and they enjoyed the fight for it. Their energy and endurance created a president as they banded together and worked tirelessly and without sleep on behalf of their friend and colleague. It was a political alliance forged by their love for their leader. Their support came from the heart. "To them it seemed as if the nation were about to lay its claim upon him"[206] and but for their dedicated, untiring, and unselfish efforts in Chicago, Abraham Lincoln might well not have traveled on the road to immortality as a "man for the ages."

William Herndon was Lincoln's law partner. Because of their close association for 16 years, he probably knew Lincoln better than any man in America in 1860. It was through Herndon's eyes the nation came to know Abraham Lincoln after his assassination. Not only was Herndon instrumental in steering Lincoln into the Republican Party, Lincoln would frequently use him as a sounding board, trying out various ideas and strategies. Herndon always called his partner "Mr. Lincoln" and he was, in turn, called "Billy" by Lincoln.[207]

Jesse Fell, a successful businessman and founder of the *Bloomington Pantagraph,* was a long-standing supporter and political friend of Lincoln. As young Whigs in the 1830s, they had boarded together when the state legislature met in Vandalia, where Lincoln was serving his first legislative term and Fell was lobbying for Bloomington interests. Later, both joined the Republican Party. Fell not only nominated Lincoln for his Senate run in 1858, but also encouraged him to run for the presidency.

Samuel Parks, Clifton Moore, Lawrence Weldon, and Oliver Davis were active members of the Eighth Circuit bar and were all Lincoln loyalists. The lawyers would ride the circuit twice yearly, usually three months at a time. During these periods court would be held at any one place from two days to a week. While on the circuit, lawyers traveled together and tried suits together and against one another.

Stephen Logan first met Abraham Lincoln in 1832. They were law partners from 1841 to 1844. After the partnership was dissolved, the two remained close political associates. In Lincoln's unsuccessful bid for a Senate seat in 1855, Logan floor-managed Lincoln's efforts and, at Lincoln's instigation, switched the votes of Lincoln's supporters to Lyman Trumbull, the ultimate winner. Lincoln's confidence in Logan was such that in Chicago, Logan had a letter from Lincoln authorizing him to withdraw Lincoln's name if it was deemed prudent.[208]

Leonard Swett, a politician and lawyer who also practiced in the Eighth Judicial Circuit, first met Lincoln in 1849. He and Lincoln shared the joys and miseries of circuit riding.[209] Lincoln and Davis had supported Swett's unsuccessful Congressional bid in 1856. When Swett won a seat in the Illinois legislature in 1858, he was a vote for Lincoln in his loss to Douglas.

John Palmer and Norman Judd had been anti-Nebraska Democrats who vigorously opposed Lincoln's 1855 Senate run. However, both became Lincoln's champions. Judd was responsible for having Chicago selected as the site of the 1860 convention. Palmer led the Lincoln charge at the Decatur convention and introduced the resolution that the Illinois delegation not only vote as a unit for Lincoln but use all honorable means to have him nominated.

Joseph Medill and Dr. Charles Ray, as owners of the *Chicago Tribune,* strongly supported Lincoln's presidential aspirations. They used their newspaper to sell Lincoln to the nation. Jesse Dubois and Lincoln served in the Illinois legislature together and had been close political associates since 1834. Richard Yates was another former Whig and had been associated with Lincoln since Yates entered the state legislature in 1842. With the support of Leonard Swett, Yates was the party's compromise gubernatorial candidate in 1860. Burton Cook was a warm supporter of Senator Wade of Ohio but, as an Illinois delegate to the convention, supported Lincoln wholeheartedly.

Orville Browning, once a Bates supporter, would lead the Lincoln charge and he became the ultimate team player in Chicago. Browning and Lincoln were social and political friends of long standing.[210] Both were in the Illinois legislature in 1836. They shared four things in common: Both were born in Kentucky; both were lawyers; both were Whigs turned Republicans; and both had been defeated by Douglas.

William Butler, Illinois state treasurer, met Lincoln when Lincoln first moved to Springfield. He greatly liked this unusual young man newly arrived from the country. Knowing Lincoln was hard up, Butler generously gave him free board at his house.[211] Theirs was a bittersweet friendship. First they had been close friends, became

Ward Hill Lamon

estranged, and then were friends again. Butler faithfully kept Lincoln apprised of what was happening at the convention.[212]

Mark Delahay, from Kansas, was an enigma and is often referred to in unflattering terms. However, Lincoln liked him and paid his expenses ($100) in Chicago.[213] Delahay made it his mission to report to Lincoln daily on the progress of the campaign.

Ward Hill Lamon, 19 years Lincoln's junior, had traveled the Eighth Judicial Circuit with Lincoln, was his partner in Danville, and had worked hard for him in both of his previous Senate races. Explained a Lincoln biographer:

> Whenever Judge Davis and the circuit riders reached Danville, Lamon felt it his duty to act as host to the travelers. After completion of the court business, when the cavalcade had assembled in Lincoln's or in the judge's hotel room, the Danville lawyer would bring in a pitcher of whiskey and bid his guests make merry. Lincoln never drank intoxicants but otherwise joined in. . . . When the whiskey had made Lamon mellow enough, he would strike up some nonsensical tune on his banjo, sing ballads, and be the life of the party.[214]

Ozias M. Hatch was the Illinois secretary of state, and in his offices Lincoln's lawyer friends assembled in January 1860 and asked Lincoln "if his name might be used at once in connection with the nomination and election."[215]

Gustave Koerner, born in Germany, was another Illinois delegate with Seward leanings. He had known Lincoln professionally and socially and was instrumental in helping Lincoln's candidacy by developing the support of foreign-born citizens.

The campaign team loved their man Lincoln, but the same was not true of their regard for each other: "Indeed, their loyalty to Lincoln was matched by the distrust they exhibited toward each other."[216] Davis would never forgive Judd for opposing Lincoln's 1855 bid for a Senate seat. In addition, Davis thought Judd had not adequately prepared for the convention when Judd failed to set up a campaign headquarters for Lincoln in Chicago.[217] Swett and Yates had been rivals for the governorship but united to defeat Judd.

Mark Delahay

In 1860, the Republican Party was still in its infancy, and there was a natural distrust between former Democrats and former Whigs and vice versa. Fell, a former Whig, disliked former Democrats and opposed Judd. Regardless, their working together for a common goal was positive proof of the primary adage of political folklore: Politics brings together strange bedfellows.

Pressing Their Advantage

The Lincoln forces were determined to capitalize on all home field advantages their campaign gained when Chicago was selected as the convention site, where Lincoln had the advantage of having the newspapers and the crowds at his beck and call. "Lincoln banners floated across every street, and buildings and omnibuses were decorated with Lincoln emblems."[218] Ray and Medill in their newspaper, the *Chicago Tribune,* ran story after story of Lincoln's qualifications and outlined the reasons he should be nominated.

Davis had a special need to produce crowds. The Republicans of Chicago, in six weeks, had constructed a large, rambling building to house the convention. The structure was christened the "Wigwam." It cost about $6,000 to build. Its capacity was in excess of 10,000 persons.[219] Davis wanted a sea of Lincoln-friendly faces in the Wigwam at all times, and he wanted them to make their presence felt.

A friendly and noisy crowd creates excitement and enthusiasm for a candidate and indicates grassroots support. In addition, a friendly and noisy crowd exerts "outside pressure" on the convention and provides the noise not only to pressure the delegates but possibly stampede the convention. Finally, and probably most important of all, belonging to a friendly and noisy Lincoln crowd would give his supporters not only the satisfaction of playing a positive role in his run for the nomination, but a stake in the outcome.

Word had been spread to Lincoln friends throughout Illinois to start moving to Chicago to help their friend and neighbor battle for the presidential nomination. Because Judd "arranged with the Chicagoans who controlled the railroads to bring in Lincoln men free of charge,"[220] the call to arms proved successful. Thousands of

Norman Judd

Lincoln supporters descended on Chicago. They roamed the city talking, arguing, and demonstrating on behalf of their good friend[221] and creating "a Lincoln atmosphere around the convention."[222]

To help with crowd control and also be faces in the friendly and noisy crowd, the Lincoln team utilized the newly-organized Wide Awake Lincoln clubs. The Wide Awakes were marching clubs. Their members were "oil-cloth-garbed, torch-carrying young men who were to parade at the rallies and in the Chicago streets as the national delegates began arriving, and who would pack the auditorium seats of the convention hall."[223]

Yet another advantage of being host to the convention was one of political intelligence. The Lincoln forces were in their own element in Chicago and "held communications with all our Illinois friends, and received regular and reliable information from all parts of the city."[224] If something was happening, Davis wanted to know the particulars.

Communications to and from the Lincoln command post in the Tremont Hotel were handled by young Republican enthusiasts. Not only did the young Republicans serve as messengers, they, along with the Wide Awakes, helped with crowd control in gathering and disseminating tickets and information and, if needed, joined the Lincoln supporters in the convention hall.

Chapter 11

Storyline Dictates Lincoln Strategy

T he storyline of the convention was if the Republicans wanted to win the White House in November, they had to carry the 11 states Fremont won in 1856 and add to that total at least three of the four crucial states—Illinois, Indiana, New Jersey, and Pennsylvania—that he failed to carry.

To Davis, this storyline not only dictated the overall Lincoln convention strategy, it also provided the formula to capture the nomination. It was almost inevitable that no Republican candidate would carry a single slave state, nor would the Southern candidate lay claim to a single free state. Victory or defeat in November hinged on the four pivotal states. Although these states were free states, "there was a chance that one or more of these . . . States might cast its vote for Douglas and popular sovereignty."[225] Therefore, the party needed a candidate who could take on Douglas in those states and win, and to Davis that was a no-brainer. "The Republican Party could not afford to lose Illinois, and there was only one Republican in Illinois who had faced Douglas and held his ground"[226]—Abraham Lincoln.

Davis realized that, in addition to Lincoln being the strongest candidate to win in Illinois, he also had all the requisites of an available, that is, widely acceptable, candidate who could win the other crucial states. As one historian noted:

> He did not have to pose as a man of the people. He was one. He had been a rail-splitter, a flatboatman, a grocery keeper, and had other

attributes common to the masses. His had been a long struggle against poverty. Even his manners, his dress, his stories and the nickname "Honest Abe" commended him to the factory worker and the farmer. His public speeches had been conservative. He had never made statements as radical as Seward's "irrepressible conflict" or "there is a higher law than the Constitution." Furthermore, he had not held public office long enough to incur the jealousies of powerful rivals.[227]

In addition, while the storyline allowed Davis to showcase Lincoln's strengths as an available candidate who could win, it also downplayed Lincoln's negatives—lack of executive experience and limited understanding of foreign policy matters. Consequently, Davis and his team focused and placed all the emphasis on how to win the presidency rather than who was most qualified to be president.

The Lincoln message had a dual theme. Davis and his team first stressed the party's need for a candidate who could carry the crucial states and then touted Lincoln as "the only candidate who had all the ingredients necessary for victory in November—who had no derogatory national image, had offended no Republican groups or factions, and had the strongest appeal in the crucial lower North."[228] In addition to being the perfect candidate, he was a proven winner. He was the only candidate who could lay claim to having defeated the Democrat's foremost candidate, Douglas; and Lincoln could bring the party what no other candidate could—the presidency.

The keys to a successful campaign are a viable strategy and clear, focused priorities. The plan developed by the Lincoln campaign team was dictated by the dynamics of 1860 convention politics. The essential starting point of the campaign was to keep Seward from being nominated on the first ballot. Davis and his team joined forces with Seward's other rivals to stop that from happening. Second, to insure that Lincoln would still be in the running after the first ballot, the team had to attract not only first ballot, but additional second and third ballot support for Lincoln. The overall goal was to make a good showing on the first ballot. They hoped by having Lincoln finish as runner-up to Seward, thus putting some distance between Lincoln and the other contenders, they could then add to Lincoln's numbers on the second and third ballots by lining up additional votes from the favorite-son states and also-rans.

The first order of business, the "Stop Seward" movement, required no formal agreement among the candidates. Instead, there was a tacit understanding or, as Judd put it, a "quiet combination," to cooperate with one another to keep Seward from getting a first ballot win,[229] "all maintaining in innumerable colloquies that Seward could not carry the state each represented."[230] If the delegates supporting other candidates and the delegates from the favorite-son states held firm and were not enticed by Weed, Seward's campaign manager, Seward could be stopped. And if Seward was unable to muster the delegates needed to nominate him on the first few ballots, his strength might crumble.

There would be no direct attacks on Seward, no confrontational tones, no innuendoes or smears, just the exploitation of his weaknesses and the placing of a radical tag on him. Paint Seward as too controversial or ideological to win the four states. Their claim, which was hammered over and over during convention week until it became a cliche, was a compelling message: Seward could not carry the doubtful states of the lower North and without them a Seward ticket was doomed to fail.

So while the opposition collectively ganged up on Seward, each candidate jockeyed and maneuvered for position as leader of the pack when Seward faltered. When that happened, the candidate who was in second place would, in all likelihood, be the one to challenge Seward and, if the opposition concentrated on him, most likely win the nomination.

For Lincoln to emerge as the compromise candidate with the acquiescence and belated support of his rivals, Davis and his team had to demonstrate to the convention that Lincoln was the most "available" candidate in 1860, that is, the one candidate who was acceptable to all factions of the party. According to a Davis biographer:

New Jersey wanted to nominate William L. Dayton, who had been candidate for vice president in 1856. Pennsylvania had paraded for Cameron. Ohio delegations were marching and shouting for their

Salmon P. Chase. Horace Greeley of the *New York Tribune* wanted Edward Bates of St. Louis. The problem before Lincoln's handful of backers was to convince these delegates that they could not nominate their candidates nor elect them if they were nominated.

Each of their candidates had glaring weaknesses. "Bates's alleged affiliation with the Know-Nothings would lose him the foreign vote. Chase was too extreme an abolitionist for moderates. Dayton was tinged with defeatism since he had lost the election for vice president in 1856."[231] And if none of them could win in November, their backers had to be convinced that no more perfect candidate could be found than Abraham Lincoln. Consequently, it was imperative Lincoln be runner-up on the first ballot. For that to happen, the Lincoln men needed more than the 22 Illinois votes and targeted those delegations they believed they could persuade to support, and commit to, him on both the first and second ballots.

The Lincoln team had to harvest the seeds that Lincoln had planted during his trips into Indiana, Ohio, New York, and New England. Everybody loved Old Abe, the Rail-Splitter. He was the ideal Republican candidate Fell had described: a man of popular origin, acknowledged ability, committed against slavery aggression, with no record to defend and no radicalism of an offensive character. In addition, he was a proven winner and there was no man in the country better equipped to fight Douglas. When, and not if, the team got its message across to the convention, Lincoln's commitment totals would rise.

In politics then, and continuing to the present, a commitment was not a binding, enforceable contract a candidate could take to the bank. A commitment was never guaranteed and, even if given, any time a delegate got a better offer he was liable to switch his allegiance. It only became a fact when the vote was actually given. A campaign manager had to determine, among other things, whether the support was firm or could be enticed away, so getting a commitment was only half the job, and the other half required the candidate to work feverishly to keep the commitment firm.

Chapter 12

The Magic Number: 233

The primal driving force behind convention politics is numbers, and for Judge Davis and his team, the magic number for nomination in 1860 was 233 votes, the delegate majority. [232] When the Lincoln team arrived in Chicago, set up shop, and began campaign operations, Seward already had about 155 votes (70 from his home state); Bates, Chase, and Cameron each had about 50 votes; and Lincoln had Illinois's 22 votes. [233] While Lincoln was low man on the totem pole, those 22 votes came from one of the doubtful states.

The total delegate count at the convention numbered 465. Of that number, about 265 were not pledged to a candidate and could vote for whomever they pleased or would be released following complimentary votes for favorite sons, who had no serious chance to win.

Those delegations coming to Chicago not pledged to a particular candidate included:

Connecticut, 12 votes
Iowa, 8 votes
Maine, 16 votes
Massachusetts, 25 votes

Indiana, 26 votes
Kentucky, 23 votes
New Hampshire, 10 votes
Virginia, 23 votes. [234]

Favorite son states included:
New Jersey, 14 votes
Pennsylvania, 54 votes

Ohio, 46 votes [235]
Vermont, 10 votes. [236]

These were the delegate pools where Davis would find the support to trigger the second part of the Lincoln formula for victory—make Lincoln runner-up to Seward on the first ballot and secure additional votes on the second and third ballot to keep Lincoln's total vote rising.

For Lincoln to be a viable player and not just another favorite-son candidate with no real chance of winning, his political base had to be expanded beyond the Illinois state borders. The team decided it would allocate little time or manpower to those states that were pledged to Seward—California, Michigan, Minnesota, and Wisconsin. Instead, Davis focused his resources on those delegates from the noncommitted states, those with favorite sons, and those states where he believed a candidate's support was not firm.

Of course, the primary goal was to garner as many votes on the first ballot as possible, or if the votes were from a favorite-son state or the state of another Seward rival, "try and get them to abandon their first choices after the initial ballot and go for Lincoln on the second and third."[237] Any increase in vote totals on subsequent ballots would demonstrate Lincoln's latent strength and overall political weight. Lincoln described his candidacy in a letter:

> My name is new in the field; and I suppose I am not the first choice of a very great many. Our policy, then, is to give no offence to others: leave them in a mood to come to us, if they shall be compelled to give up their first love.[238]

A simple plan to implement—make friends in all delegations and enemies in none—and Davis set it in motion on the first day. The plan required the Lincoln team to establish a personal connection with the delegates from other states. Davis assigned individual members of his staff to shepherd a particular delegation. For the most part, geography dictated his selection. If a team member had roots in another state, he appointed that member to keep vigil over the delegates from his former state. Parks, who was born in Vermont, headed the group to monitor the Vermont delegates.[239] Swett, from Maine, was assigned to bird-dog the Maine delegation.[240] Medill, who hailed from Ohio, met and worked with the Ohio delegation.[241] Stephen Logan and Richard Yates, from the Bluegrass state, tended the Kentucky delegation.[242] Ward Lamon, who had spent his boyhood in western Virginia, shadowed the Virginia delegation.[243] And William Dole, a member of the Illinois delegation who formerly lived in Indiana, was the liaison with the Hoosiers.[244]

A shepherd was expected to greet and mingle with his old friends and neighbors, eat and drink with them, answer questions, soothe egos, tend to their needs, and then—and this was the key—tell them the amazing story of Abraham Lincoln: "Birth in a log cabin, practically no schooling, worked as a farm hand, split rails, took a flat boat to New Orleans, educated himself."[245]

In addition to their assigned duties, the shepherds were expected to regularly report to Davis any movement, good or bad, within that particular delegation. He kept a running delegate total going. As the commanding general of the Lincoln forces, "The judge himself sat behind a table at headquarters, received their reports and urged them on to greater efforts."[246] The judge had his own inimitable style in assessing the information—good news would be greeted with a placid grunt and bad news with an angry snort.[247] Occasionally, Davis "sallied out to argue for Lincoln with a group of delegates."[248] If a particular state delegation wanted to hear about Lincoln, Davis assigned Browning and Swett to make the presentation and sometimes he accompanied them.[249] He was confident that once personal contact was made and the delegations heard the Lincoln sales pitch, Lincoln's first, second, and third ballot numbers would increase.

Davis was keenly aware that many delegations were coming to the convention uncommitted to any particular candidate and were ready to barter their votes. In 1860 it was customary "for the managers of candidates to make pledges in exchange for votes at national conventions."[250] A state delegation quickly learned that a bloc vote for a candidate greatly enhanced its negotiating power when seeking favors.

The first targeted delegation was Indiana. Lincoln had grown up in Indiana and had many political friends there. His debates with

Douglas in 1858 had attracted widespread attention in the state and many crossed the border into Illinois to listen and cheer him on. In the debate at Charleston, Illinois, an Indiana band led the Lincoln parade.[251]

More important, he had received a letter in late April from an Indiana friend who indicated that Indiana's support was up for grabs and would go to the highest bidder.[252] Being warmly disposed toward Lincoln, Indiana gave him the first chance to do business. Though distasteful to Lincoln, he thought about it, made his decision, and replied that his representatives would meet the delegation when they arrived in Chicago.[253]

On Saturday, May 12, Davis, as arranged by Lincoln, met with the Indiana delegation, probably in the Tremont Hotel, where the Indiana and Illinois delegations were quartered. It was a *quid pro quo* bargaining session, which, unfortunately, is still a viable expedient in politics today. It was actually a win-win situation for both sides and, like all political *quid pro quo* arrangements, was contingent on Lincoln winning. If Lincoln did not win the nomination, Indiana got nothing.

Indiana, knowing its votes were crucial to the success of Lincoln's efforts, wanted, and Davis is alleged by some to have pledged, two offices—secretary of the interior and commissioner of Indian affairs—for its united support.[254] Caleb Smith was purportedly promised the cabinet post and Dole would become the commissioner. However, before the deal was consummated, the Indiana delegation had to be convinced Lincoln was a winner. While they took the matter under consideration, they probably shopped around for a better offer.[255]

Letters and telegrams from team members and supporters, beginning on May 13 and running through May 17, 1860, kept Lincoln apprised of what was happening in Chicago. Reading between the lines, these communications provided the most telling insights of the progress of the campaign. In a letter from Dubois, dated May 13, Lincoln was informed that Indiana was leaning to him "although a portion are for Bates." Eight of the Ohio men favored him. Horace Greeley was working for Edward

Bates and not Senator Seward. Pennsylvania was playing hardball for Cameron, Iowa felt like going for him on the first ballot, and Massachusetts indicated it was for success of the party rather than the success of a particular candidate. Lincoln was also informed that John Wentworth, who had been denied a position in the Illinois delegation, was for him today but "in good faith cannot tell what he may do tomorrow."[256]

On Monday, May 14, Indiana came on board the Lincoln bandwagon, more than doubling his first ballot total to 48 votes.[257] As likely as not, the prospective office holders, Smith and Dole, helped persuade the delegation to come to Lincoln as a unit.

With Indiana's support, Lincoln was a bona fide player in the presidential sweepstakes. If Ohio's eight votes were added to his roster, he had moved from last to second in the delegate count with 56 commitments, a good base from which to build.

Once on board, the Indiana delegation provided the Lincoln team with a great deal more than their collective votes. First, the delegate support came from another state that was crucial to the Republican's success in November. Two of the four battleground states were now firmly in the Lincoln column. Second, the Indiana delegates became active members of the Lincoln team and worked tirelessly for his nomination. From the moment they signed on, the Indiana delegates worked shoulder to shoulder with the Illinois delegates to convince other delegates that Lincoln was a winner and urged them to join the swelling ranks of a man who was likely to be the next president.

Indiana's nominee for governor, Henry Lane, initially thought that McLean would have been the strongest candidate in his state and that Bates had the qualifications to be president. When he found the contest was between Seward and Lincoln, he worked tirelessly for Lincoln "as if life itself depended upon success."[258] Lane, according to various Lincoln biographers, "was an extremely influential man who had great weight with the delegates because four years before he had been permanent chairman of the Party's first National Convention, in which capacity he had won national celebrity by delivering a fiery speech."[259] He spent hours "skipping round from one delegation to another," spreading his message "that with Seward as the candidate Indiana would be lost, while Lincoln's nomination would save the state."[260] Lane shared Lincoln's views on slavery and was, like Lincoln, a former Whig and a great admirer of Henry Clay. He advocated, as did Lincoln, the non-extension of slavery and at the same time, the non-interference with slavery in the states where it existed.[261]

Enlightening Reports

Six letters were sent to Lincoln on May 14 which detailed the efforts of his campaign team and supporters. Ray confidently reported that Lincoln's first ballot support would not be confined to Illinois and would increase after that, and that he would rather have Lincoln's "chances than those of any other man."[262] Butler, in two letters, informed Lincoln his chances were brightening; that Illinois, Indiana, Iowa, Maine, and New Hampshire would present a solid front for him; that Ohio and Pennsylvania were divided, with Ohio leaning toward him; that the New York and Pennsylvania delegations were fighting and both wanted Lincoln as vice president on a ticket headed by Seward or Cameron, respectively; and that things looked bright and all spoke of him as their second choice.[263]

Delahay advised that things "are working admirably well now;" that Lincoln's stock was rising; Indiana was all right; New York and Pennsylvania were quarreling; Ohio was prepared to do a good part after Chase, Ohio's favorite son, had his compliments paid him; New Hampshire and a part of New Jersey were talking for Lincoln as was Massachusetts; all conceded he could easily be nominated for vice president; and the Lincoln team was not pressing his claims too hard and was making friends everywhere.[264]

Nathan M. Knapp, a former member of the Illinois General Assembly, sent Lincoln an encouraging report, that things were working, and that the team was laboring to make Lincoln the "second choice of all the Delegations we can where we cannot make you first choice." To accomplish their goal, he reported that they "are dealing tenderly with delegates, taking them in detail, and making no fuss."[265]

In many of the states other candidates might be the first choice, but Lincoln was the unconditional second choice of all. The strategy proved so successful that Palmer later claimed the biggest struggle of the campaign was to prevent Lincoln's nomination for vice president, reporting that the Seward men, who wanted and were determined to have Lincoln fill the second slot, literally overwhelmed the Lincoln team with kindness.[266]

Amos Tuck, a New Hampshire delegate, advised Lincoln his nomination was "within the range of decided possibilities," and that he was working on New England delegates. He also cautioned Lincoln not to be misled by their first votes; they (New England) would come in on time.[267] As noted earlier, Tuck was a true Lincoln friend who, at the 1856 Republican Convention, had the satisfaction, on the call of New Hampshire, to name Abraham Lincoln for vice president. Now, four years later, he was again hard at work for his friend.

With at least 56 or more delegates in his pocket, Lincoln's prospects suddenly looked more promising. If he could add to his base strength another 40 to 50 votes it could put him second to Seward, and far ahead of the other candidates. If so, he would stand as the candidate to challenge Seward.

Once Indiana came on board the Lincoln Express, Davis decided to try his luck in the Northeast. He wanted to sound out the loyalties for Seward in the area and, at the same time, test the reservoir of good fellowship Lincoln had accumulated on his recent speaking tour in New England. While Seward and Weed had worked New England hard to add them to Seward's roster, and Weed had contributed money to New Hampshire Republicans for elections,[268] the New England delegations, for the most part, came to the convention uninstructed and could vote for their candidate of choice.

Though leaning toward Seward, the New Englanders came to the table thinking of the greater good of getting a Republican elected to the White House in 1860, and they wanted a "man who could make victory certain."[269] They felt the convention choice should not be a particular candidate but the candidate who could carry the four doubtful states. In short, their view was that expediency should trump principle and experience, that the convention should "pick the best candidate—the man who most certainly can win —rather than the best President."[270]

This was fantastic news for Davis and the Lincoln campaign. It moved the debate from who was the most qualified man for the presidency to who could win the four crucial states. Now, with a little prodding by Davis and his team, the New England delegates could connect the dots and reach the conclusion that one man, and one man only, could win all four crucial states—Abraham Lincoln. Davis could not have asked for more. The opportunity to cut into Seward's strength in that area was well worth the effort, even if they failed.

On Tuesday, May 15, Davis, Browning, and delegate Thomas Marshall had a meeting with the Maine and New Hampshire delegations.[271] Browning, a member of the Illinois delegation, led the team effort with the New Englanders. Although Browning had once been a Bates supporter, he was assigned the task of convincing the delegates that Lincoln, and not Bates or Seward, could win the crucial states.

Davis and his team were unaware the Maine delegation had been instructed by one of its leaders, Senator Hannibal Hamlin, to contact the delegates from the four crucial states and determine the candidate they thought could carry those states. Nor were they aware of the results: while some thought Seward could win, the majority thought Lincoln was the man. Following that rationale, not only did the Lincoln team get a warm reception from the two delegations, they won promises of first ballot votes.[272] Apparently their efforts and Tuck's influence were beginning to pay off. The New Englanders were beginning to connect the dots.

That evening, Davis received word from Massachusetts requesting a visit. He and Browning responded, with Browning addressing them "upon the aspect of political affairs in Illinois."[273] Although they were not able to swing any votes for Lincoln, the meeting was not unsuccessful. The next day the chairman of the delegation,

John A. Andrew, wanting a Republican victory in November more than his personal preference (Seward) decided that Lincoln was the man to lead the coalition against Seward. He organized a band of New Englanders and made the rounds of the other delegations advancing Lincoln's cause.[274]

The Lincoln campaign was gaining momentum daily. Davis and Dubois telegraphed Lincoln on May 15 that they were quietly "moving heaven & Earth" and that the heart of the delegates was for him. In their opinion nothing would beat them but "old fogy [sic] politicians."[275] Dubois also telegraphed that Lincoln's prospects were very good, that the team was acting nobly and doing everything to garner the nomination, and that Orville Browning was "doing his duty" and becoming a true Lincoln team player.[276]

Butler and Delahay each sent a letter to Lincoln dated May 15. Butler reported about a confidential meeting he had with a New Yorker, supposedly with the blessing of Seward's campaign manager, Weed. If Lincoln would agree to take second spot on a Seward ticket, $100,000 would be placed in proper hands for the campaigns in Illinois and Indiana. Butler's reply to the New Yorker was that under no circumstances would Lincoln take second spot.[277]

Delahay reported the New York delegation came in great numbers and had a headquarters in every hotel. A straw vote on a train from Columbus gave 73 votes for Seward, 65 for Lincoln, 15 for Chase, 10 for Bates, 4 for McLean and 50 for Douglas. A disgruntled John Wentworth asserted in his newspaper that Illinois could be carried by Seward or by Lincoln. Delahay thought Wentworth was a "dog, and unworthy to be called a member of our party." Further, Delahay wrote it was rumored that the Texas delegates and two-thirds of the Virginia delegation were for Seward; that New York and Pennsylvania were still quarreling as were Weed and Greeley; and New York made a run at the Bates delegates with a vice presidency for Francis B. Blair, Jr.[278]

Wentworth, resentful of not being selected as an Illinois delegate, was creating the mischief Lincoln feared. He had a banner stretched across his newspaper office proclaiming "Seward for President," and he was going about the convention talking openly for Seward. Wentworth's open support of Seward and his newspaper's claim that Seward could win in Illinois, one of the crucial states, was undermining the Lincoln claim that Seward could not carry the doubtful states. Davis was concerned enough about Wentworth's activities to have someone follow him around and respond to, and neutralize, his claims.[279]

Chapter 13

Second and Third Ballot Support

A long with its first ballot efforts, the Lincoln team also aggressively went after second and third ballot support and targeted not only those delegates from the favorite-son states—New Jersey, Ohio, Pennsylvania, and Vermont—but also from those states pledged to, but not strongly for, Bates: Connecticut, Delaware, and Maryland. Vermont, with its 10 votes, bought the Lincoln sales pitch and promised to come to Lincoln after the first ballot.[280]

However, Weed, Seward's campaign manager, had beaten the Lincoln men to New Jersey and there was no breakthrough.[281] Weed had convinced New Jersey the dream ticket of Seward-Lincoln could carry Illinois and Indiana. To counter, Davis had Palmer speak to the delegation about the improbability of the success of the proposed dream ticket in Illinois. Palmer's argument, persuasive yet unheeded, was that in Illinois former Democrats turned Republicans would never support two ex-Whigs for the top spots.[282] Ironically, Palmer was the same man who so vigorously opposed Lincoln in 1855 in his bid for a Senate seat and his argument in Chicago was entirely consistent with his earlier opposition to Lincoln—former Democrats had a natural distrust for former Whigs.

Ohio, with 46 votes, was the third-largest delegation. While it was divided, with Salmon Chase expected to get most of the first ballot votes as its favorite son, the delegation stood united against

Seward. In fact, one Ohioan lamented that "with Seward the leader the Republicans would remain in the wilderness longer than the children of Israel under Moses. . . ."[283] As reported to him, and as proved to be true, Lincoln had at least eight true friends in the delegation.[284] His mail from Ohio also indicated there was no strong attachment to Chase,[285] that he (Lincoln) would get some first ballot votes, and after a ballot or two, Chase's support would dwindle to less than a quarter of Ohio's 48 votes. The Lincoln team (Delahay, Butler) felt, with Chase aside, Lincoln was the choice of Ohio, and that Lincoln vote totals after the first ballot would increase, but by just how much was uncertain.[286]

Pennsylvania was the crown jewel of the favorite-son states with 54 votes. However, the Pennsylvania delegates were not looking for any deals. Instead, upon their arrival, they were offering deals and trying to generate support for their favorite son, Simon Cameron.[287] They came to the convention 600 strong and expected the convention to give Cameron serious consideration since Pennsylvania was the largest of the four doubtful states.[288] The total votes of the other three doubtful states—Illinois, Indiana, and New Jersey—was 62, only eight more than Pennsylvania's vote total. While Cameron's supporters were beating the bushes for support during the pre-convention campaigning, they found no takers. Even so, they consistently maintained their opposition to Seward for the nomination. Davis believed once the Pennsylvanians came to the conclusion Cameron was unable to generate any outside emotion among the delegates, they would be ready to explore other alternatives and possibly strike a bargain.

Edward Bates's strength supposedly came from Connecticut, Maryland, and Delaware. The Lincoln team had let Greeley carry the ball for Bates against Seward in those states. Their strategy in pursuing support was indirect—no promises, only whispers.[289] They were now looking for second-ballot support and dropped hints about possible cabinet posts and having a place at the White House table when Lincoln was elected. Delaware bought the Lincoln spiel and agreed to come over to him on the second ballot.

There were a number of delegations from states with no formal Republican Party organizations. These were fertile battleground for all candidates. Kentucky was represented with a 23-man delegation; Texas with a 6-man delegation; and Virginia a 23-man delegation.[290] While it was expected Seward would get the support of the Texas delegation through Weed's manipulations,[291] Davis actively pursued members of the Kentucky and Virginia delegations and assigned team members to shepherd their activities, arguing primarily that the party must nominate Lincoln if it was to win in November. The Virginians were unorganized and they readily made promises of support, not only to Davis but to Weed as well.[292]

To get the support of Kentucky, the Lincoln team again not only whispered and hinted that a cabinet post might be in the offing for support, but also stressed Lincoln's ties to the state, Lincoln having been born in Kentucky.[293] Davis sensed movement and expected to get some first-ballot votes from both Kentucky and Virginia. Overall, the Lincoln team was making significant headway. Their message was starting to impact the convention as the number of commitments to Lincoln was steadily increasing.

On May 15, 1860, convention eve, the lead article in the *Chicago Tribune* gave eight reasons why Lincoln should be nominated. Titled "The Winning Man—Abraham Lincoln," the article pointed out Lincoln had never sought the office; he radiated the fundamentals of Republicanism on slavery; he was solid on all other Republican issues; he was not sectional; because of his humble beginnings he was a man of the people; he never associated with the Know Nothings; he was honest; and, finally, he could be elected if nominated.[294] Lincoln was the man who could not fail to win for the party.

Thurlow Weed

Chapter 14

Thurlow Weed Heads the Seward Team

During this period before the start of the convention, the Seward forces were not sitting idle but trying to woo enough first-ballot support to end the suspense. Seward had gone home to Auburn, New York, to await word from Chicago of his nomination and prepare his acceptance speech. He would be 59 on May 16, the day the convention opened, and, expecting his nomination as a birthday present, he postponed his celebration for two days and invited a large number of guests to attend a gala celebration at his home. His neighbors in Auburn were also confident of his success and had rented a pair of cannons to use at his belated birthday party. When fired, the cannons would announce his nomination.[295]

Thurlow Weed, called Lord Thurlow by his friends, represented Seward in Chicago. He was a veteran of many political wars and convention politics, first as a Whig and now as a Republican. He was reputed to know the mysteries of convention politics better than any man living in 1860. Never an officeholder, he was the power behind the throne and recognized as a supreme power broker and kingmaker. Weed was the man behind Seward in the latter's campaigns for governor and senator.[296] In May of 1860 he came to Chicago with one purpose only: to secure for his friend, Senator William Henry Seward, the Republican nomination for president.

For years, Seward, Weed, and Horace Greeley, publisher of the *New York Tribune,* controlled New York politics. However, in 1854, in a letter not made public at the time and its contents guarded, Greeley had voluntarily opted out of the political triumvirate, withdrawing because he felt he had not been afforded the proper recognition nor the political rewards he believed he deserved. With Greeley out, Seward and Weed took up the slack and retained control of New York politics. When the New York delegates to Chicago were selected, Greeley was left out.[297]

Weed was a tall, suave, gracious man and, while in Chicago, he held court in the Richmond House, holding day-long receptions for the delegates who either dropped by or were brought in. As soon as he arrived, he "began serving champagne and cigars to delegates from Maine to California while assuring them with backslaps that Seward was sure to win."[298] Even though he stayed in his suite and seldom ventured out, Weed knew everything that was going on in every delegation.[299] He was the consummate politician. When a delegation visited his headquarters, he usually surprised the delegates when he called them by name and chatted with them like old friends.[300]

Although a national campaign could be expensive, money was no object to the New Yorker. Weed had plenty, and if he needed more he knew where to get it. He strongly believed the ends justified the means and he lavishly spread money to wine, dine, and entertain the delegates.

The theme of the Seward campaign was not on how to win the presidency. Instead it centered on how the presidency should be run and the qualities a president in 1860 should possess. Weed outlined those qualities to his visitors over cigars and champagne. He reminded his listeners that four years before, the party had nominated John C. Fremont, who had no qualifications for the presidency, and the party lost. The lesson to be learned from the defeat was that the Republican candidate must be a man with executive ability, a man of real statesmanlike qualities, well-known throughout the country, and experienced in national affairs. He claimed the one and only man who possessed all those qualities was Seward.[301]

So, although Seward's campaign theme did not directly attack Lincoln, it did so indirectly by questioning Lincoln's fitness to govern, and implying that Lincoln was too inexperienced to run the country.[302]

When Weed arrived in Chicago, he heard the chorus message of Seward's rivals that his man could not win the four doubtful states, that the party needed to nominate an available candidate who could unite all factions of the party and win the four states. Although unsettling, Weed didn't believe their claims were fatal to Seward's candidacy. He mapped out a strategy for refuting their assertions and quickly put it into operation. Weed countered first by claiming, with Seward—and only Seward—at the top of the ticket, money would be no problem; they had enough money to mount and wage a victorious campaign in the doubtful states.[303] When that didn't work, he unsuccessfully tried to persuade the gubernatorial candidates in Indiana and Pennsylvania to throw their support to Seward. If they did he would provide them with the wherewithal to win their races.[304]

Then, when Weed found Lincoln much stronger than he anticipated, he tried to knock him out of the presidential race by putting the Illinois favorite son on the ticket as Seward's running mate. A Seward-Lincoln dream ticket would also throw water on the doubtful state theory advanced by Seward foes.[305] When the Lincoln men refused his overtures, Weed tried to persuade the convention to draft Lincoln as Seward's running mate.[306] Meanwhile, determined to cover all possible contingencies to insure Seward's nomination, Weed made a run at the Bates supporters with a promise of a vice presidency for Frank Blair of Missouri.[307]

Seward was far ahead of the field. The best strategy against the united opposition was to win the nomination on the first or second ballots. If the opposition could not agree on their choice or waited too long to close ranks behind their choice, Seward, he felt, would win with ease. "A mere 50 votes would almost do it; to gather that many from the supply of 150 seemed no difficult matter." Although Weed's goal was to corner enough new votes from the delegate pool to end all confusion by getting Seward nominated on the first ballot, he felt certain he could, if necessary, get the votes needed on the second ballot.[308]

Weed had worked on the New Jersey delegation. He was confident Pennsylvania would throw its support to Seward on the second ballot. Seward had earlier journeyed to Harrisburg, Pennsylvania, and met with Cameron and the Pennsylvania legislature. Seward, who boasted that Cameron's friends were his friends, had told them what they wanted to hear regarding a protective tariff to help the state's manufacturers compete and he left with some faint whispers of support. Later Cameron requested a meeting with Weed in either Philadelphia or Washington, but the two never got together.[309] However, according to Weed biographer Glyndon G. Van Deusen, "Weed urged Cameron to have a friend at Chicago with whom he could confer"[310] and Cameron's friend, Alexander Cumming, had promised Weed that "Pennsylvania would be kept in the field until Weed could again interview its leaders."[311]

Weed also was aware Seward had personally visited with Maryland leaders and had dropped hints of political plums if he was successful. Furthermore, it was rumored that some of the Illinois delegates were leaning to Seward and might shift to him on the second ballot. Regardless, Weed was confident; as an old campaigner, he felt he could deliver.

When the Republican National Committee met in December 1859 to decide on the site of the 1860 convention, Weed had tried to have it held in a city in New York, his ballpark, but was unsuccessful. Going into a strange and hostile environment in a political campaign had its disadvantages, but he had been there before and knew what he had to do. Weed prided himself that he was able to improvise.

Later, when Weed became aware that a building was being constructed in Chicago to house the convention, a building far larger than anything that had been needed in the past, which would hold 10,000 people, far more than necessary, he thought it possible the Illinois Republicans were trying to pack the convention hall with supporters for their favorite son. When this information was coupled with a report he received in March from an Ohio supporter that Illinois was trying to organize the opposition to block Seward's nomination,[312] Weed became concerned. To "make sure that Chicago would hear plenty of Seward noise"[313] and be well represented and possibly stampede the convention, he brought his support with him. New York came to the convention with 13 railroad cars full of "irrepressibles."

The New York contingent, more than 2,000 strong, "were vociferous, aggressive, boisterous, and they brought with them from New York outsiders and workers and brass bands who filled the streets with processions and the nights with music to such an extent that the Seward enthusiasm seemed tumultuous and all-absorbing."[314] One noted historian referred to this new breed, the outsiders and workers, as "a motley crowd of men hired to march and to cheer for particular candidates—a kind of out-of-door claque which did not wait for a point to be made in favor of its man, but went off in rounds of applause at the mere mention of his name."[315]

The New Yorkers who descended on Chicago often expressed their opinion lustily and referred to Republicans they did not care for in unkind and profane expressions, especially those thought to be conservative. Greeley was not well liked by the group. The mildest epithet used for him was that Greeley was "a d——d old ass."[316] On the train to Chicago, they consumed large quantities of whiskey and other ardent beverages and enjoyed singing songs not found in hymnbooks.[317]

When the New Yorkers arrived in Chicago, they marched to their headquarters at the Richmond House to the commands of Tom Hyer, a noted New York prizefighter and gambler. Hyer was in charge of marshalling the Seward forces and leading the marching and cheering. Because of his ability to mix the most alluring drinks known to New York City, Hyer had charge of the special barroom at the Richmond House[318] and, over champagne and cigars, was jokingly referred to as Seward's "Hyer Law."[319]

Parenthetically, the Lincoln team, after they became aware of the large number of supporters from New York and Pennsylvania that had descended on Chicago, had to counter the countermove and "succeeded in getting together fully 10,000 men from Illinois and Indiana, ready to march, shout, or fight for Lincoln."[320]

Carl Schurz, a delegate from Wisconsin and a Seward man, "First, last, and all the time,"[321] described how the Seward headquarters conducted its operations. Soon after the Wisconsin delegation arrived in Chicago, it reported to the Richmond House to get suggestions on how they could help their candidate. Instead of finding the more distinguished members of the New York delegation holding court, they found Weed surrounded by politicians of a "lower sort," riffraff who had been brought to do Weed's legwork. These men talked freely about the services they had rendered or were going to render. They had marched in parades and carried Seward banners, trying to create the impression the whole country wanted Seward. They entertained the delegations with "no end of champagne and cigars, to win them for Seward."[322] For those who could help the Seward cause, they hinted proper "recognition" if they won. "Among these men Weed moved as the great captain, with ceaseless activity and noiseless step, receiving their reports and giving new instructions in his peculiar whisper, now and then taking one into a corner of the room for a secret talk, or disappearing with another through a side door for transactions still more secret."[323]

A Man of Influence

There was one influential New Yorker who came to the convention not as a delegate from New York but from Oregon.[324] Although he "was working rather to defeat Seward than to nominate Lincoln,"[325] his appearance provided all Seward rivals with a fortuitous stroke of good luck. Horace Greeley was the founder and publisher of the most important Republican newspaper in the land, the *New York Tribune*. The *Tribune* was more than a New York newspaper. "Its weekly edition had a national circulation of 200,000" and its "popularity in the rural districts of the West caused Bayard Taylor, a writer of the period, to declare that it 'comes next to the Bible.'"[326] In fact, according to Lincoln biographers, Greeley was reputed as being "the greatest single journalistic influence in the country,"[327] and "was one of the men whose opinion counted

Horace Greeley

for most in the minds of the delegates from the country,"[328] and was as influential as a state delegation.[329]

While Greeley had for 14 years been a member of the in-group of three, which included Seward and Weed and controlled New York politics, he was now an outsider looking in. After Greeley had abruptly withdrawn from the political partnership, the remaining partners thought the partnership could survive without him, that they didn't need him.

Although his former political partners excluded him from the New York delegation, Greeley was bound and determined to be a force—and not a bystander—at the convention. By pulling strings, he "was chosen by the Oregon delegation as a substitute for a delegate from that territory who had not been able to spare the time or money to attend."[330] As a delegate, Greeley not only had a vote in the convention and was assigned to the Resolutions Committee,[331] he also had the freedom to walk around on the convention floor at will, mingling with the other delegates as an equal and, more important, "itching to do battle with the New York leaders on the convention floor."[332]

On his way to the convention, Greeley had stopped off at Albany to visit with Weed. The stopover lasted for a day or so. When Greeley reboarded the train to continue his journey to Chicago, Weed had the impression Greeley was going to support Seward's candidacy.[333] Impressions to the contrary, payback time was at hand. Greeley arrived in Chicago with a single purpose: to crusade against the nomination of Seward, "fighting him with all the intensity of his nature and all the resources at his command."[334] Greeley became a "stop-Seward operator."[335]

The dissolution of the political partnership of Seward, Weed, and Greeley was important convention news. Numerous flyers placed in all the hotels spread news of the imbroglio in the New York delegation: "Greeley at the Tremont, Weed at the Richmond House."[336] As soon as he had arrived in Chicago, Greeley went about his independent campaign against Seward, interviewing the early arrivals. During the three-day period before the convention opened, "he was to be seen in every hotel lobby and state headquarters, easily identifiable with his moon face, drooping specs, and loose-hanging, rumpled clothes, buttonholing delegations with amiable, short speeches."[337] However, when the paths of Greeley and Weed crossed in Chicago, ". . . Weed would stride past him—suave, smiling, pretending not to notice."[338]

"It was only necessary for someone to say in a rough but friendly way, 'There's old Greeley,' and all within hearing distance grouped about him. Not infrequently the two or three to whom he began speaking increased until that which had started as a conversation ended as a speech."[339]

Believing Seward "could not carry the middle-of-the-roaders, the moderates, the waverers, the border states,"[340] Greeley had a modus operandi not to attack Seward directly or say any unkind words about him. Instead, his pitch was that Seward could not be elected even if nominated; the Republican Party was a sectional party and it had no strength outside of the North; and in order to win, it had to have the entire North, but there were a number of states in the North that would not go for Seward. For those skeptical delegations, Greeley, to corroborate his claims, would produce politicians from the doubtful states to relate their own stories of concern and probable defeat if Seward headed the ticket.[341]

On the eve of the convention, May 15, 1860, the Lincoln forces got another shot of luck. On that evening Thurlow Weed had rented the Wigwam to stage an elaborate event to drum up support for Seward, inviting the public to hear pro-Seward speakers lavish praise on his man. The purpose was to demonstrate that not only was Seward loved, but that he had the rousing support of the people. Weed envisioned a tremendous celebration, but his plan was foiled when it was detected by the opposition and a delegate from Pennsylvania, William D. "Pig Iron" Kelley. An ardent Cameron supporter, Kelley, on the pretense of offering a routine motion, gained the floor and refused to relinquish it. His one-man filibuster continued until midnight when the bored crowd had dwindled down from 12,000 to less than 1,000.[342]

THE REPUBLICAN WIGWAM.

Erected by the Republicans of Chicago for the use of the Republican Convention.

Dedicated May 12th 1860. —✴— *Capable of holding 10,000 Persons.*

Published by JONES, PERDUE & SMALL, Stationers, No. 122 Lake. St. Chicago. Ill.ˢ

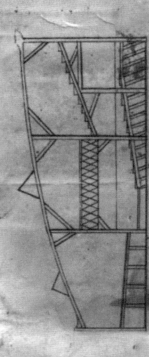

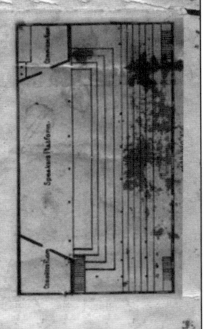

Chapter 15

The Call to Order

At 12:10 p.m. on Wednesday, May 16, 1860, in Chicago, Illinois, the Republican National Convention was called to order by Governor E.D. Morgan of New York.[343] For the three unforgettable days of its existence it was, without any doubt, "a grand spectacle."[344] It was a universe of its own, and during its brief life cycle it gave birth to more emotions and drama than its creators ever imagined. The events and happenings that transpired in Chicago during those three days evolved into the template of convention protocol that all future political conventions would religiously imitate.

On opening day the Wigwam was filled to capacity of 10,000, with another 20,000 to 30,000 standing outside trying to witness history in the making. The builders had taken advantage of the grade of the streets to construct a series of wide platforms or landings on the main floor, descending from the main entrance to the orchestra pit directly below the speakers' platform. These landings permitted a seated audience to easily see the platform and were reserved for alternates and holders of special tickets distributed by the delegates. Running around three sides of the building was a gallery which seated about 3,000 persons; it was reserved for ladies and the gentlemen who accompanied them. Although the inside of the building was left rough and not planed, the Republican ladies of Chicago lent their efforts and decorated the interior with paintings, statuaries, and wreaths.[345]

The speakers' platform ran the width of the building, and at each end of the stage were committee rooms for caucusing purposes. The remainder of the platform housed the delegates, segregated by state. Although more than 900 newspapermen applied for seats on the platform, only 60 newspaper correspondents could be accommodated.[346] The location of each state delegation was identified by a standard with a placard bearing the state name. The acoustics in the building were perfect and a speaker could not only be easily seen by all but heard with no difficulty in all parts of the building.[347]

An elegant and costly standard, courtesy of the Young Men's Republican Club of New York, hung on the west end of the stage. "It bore its blazoned stars and legend, all complete, save for two blanks following the lines, For President_____ For Vice-President_____. These blanks, said a *Chicago Tribune* article, 'were eloquent with a purpose, the purpose of the entire convention, all ready for the campaign but *waiting for the names*.'"[348]

The convention in Chicago provided five firsts. It was:

- the first convention to be held in Chicago,
- the first to have a building constructed for its use,
- the first to install telegraph wires and instruments for use by the reporters covering the convention,
- the first to admit the general public to view its sessions, and
- the first to exploit the custom of cheering and counter-cheering in tests of noise and endurance at political conventions.

"At half past eleven the three 20-foot doors on Market street were opened, slowly at first and only to ticket holders, and the tide began to flow past the doorkeepers." As soon as the ticket holders were in, the barriers were removed and the crowd rushed in and completely filled the hall.[349] "The standing room, holding 4,500 persons, was packed in about five minutes"[350] and they, too, were able to see and hear all the proceedings.[351] When the meeting was called to order, it was before "the largest audience that had ever assembled within doors in the country."[352]

Without a special ticket, the best seats were in the balcony where the action could be easily seen and clearly heard. There was, however, a little catch. The balcony had chairs that could accommodate about 3,000 people but, as previously noted, was reserved for ladies who were accompanied by gentlemen. This, of course, created quite a demand for feminine escorts, and with a little bartering, a man could get a good seat and the lady, if she so desired, could exit the building and help another man gain entry. "[S]chool girls were found in the street and given a quarter each to see a gentleman safely in. Other girls, those of undoubted character were much sought after as escorts. One of them being asked to take a gentleman to the gallery and offered a half dollar for so doing, excused herself by saying she had already taken two men in at each of the three doors and was afraid of arrest if she carried the enterprise any further."[353] For other females, however, it was a different story. An Indian squaw selling moccasins was pressed into service, but her young Republican escort was denied entry because the policeman unilaterally decided that she was no lady.[354]

The scene was very picturesque and animated. There were hundreds of women, wearing the high-peaked, flower-filled bonnets and bright shawls and plaids of the day, sitting in the gallery. Below on the platform were seated many of the notable men of the United States—William M. Evarts, Thomas Corwin, Carl Schurz, David Wilmot, Thaddeus Stevens, Joshua Giddings, George William Curtis, Francis P. Blair and his two sons, Andrew H. Reeder, George Ashmun, Gideon Welles, Preston King, Cassius M. Clay, Gratz Brown, George S. Boutwell, and Thurlow Weed.[355]

Numerous representatives of the press were on hand. They included Horace Greeley, Samuel Bowles, Murat Halstead, Isaac H. Bromley, Joseph Medill, Horace White, Joseph Hawley, Henry Villard, and A.K. McClure.[356]

As the convention host delegation, Illinois was responsible for the physical arrangements of the convention, including the printing and distribution of special tickets needed to get into the convention hall and the placement of the state delegations on the convention floor. Here, too, the Lincoln team seized the opportunity to use its host status as a leverage to gain an edge over its rivals. First, special care was taken to see that the Lincoln supporters were supplied with tickets before tickets were distributed to others.[357] Hundreds of lower-floor convention tickets were passed out to members of the Wide Awake Lincoln clubs.[358]

Second, Judd was responsible for arranging the seating of the state delegations in the convention hall, and he configured the seating arrangements that maximized Illinois's control of the convention floor and minimized the New York delegation's sphere of influence so it would not spread to other delegations. Aided by Medill, Judd seated the New York delegates at one end of the hall and surrounded them with delegates from other states that favored Seward. The delegates from Pennsylvania, Ohio, and other doubtful states, whose votes would in all likelihood be decisive, were placed at the other end of the hall between the Illinois and Indiana delegates. The seating configuration gave the Lincoln forces free access to these delegates. At the same time, they would be nearly inaccessible to New York representatives.[359]

The permanent chairman of the convention was elected and the honor went to George Ashmun[360] of Massachusetts, thought to be a Seward supporter.[361] He proved to be an excellent presiding officer and his clear, full-toned voice was refreshing to hear amid the clamor of the convention.[362]

A chair that was placed on the platform for his use was donated by Michigan and it was the first chair made in that state. It was an armchair of the most primitive description, stump-like, the seat dug out of an immense log and mounted on large rockers. Another chair, especially made for the occasion, was a chair constructed of 34 kinds of wood, each piece from a different state or territory.[363] "As a symbol of authority, the chairman was presented with a gavel made from a piece of oak taken from Commodore Perry's flag-ship, the *Lawrence*."[364]

Wine, Women, and Caucuses

The first two days of the convention were devoted to acceptance of delegates, other organizational business, and the drafting of the platform. The delegates spent the evenings caucusing, drinking and partying, and whatever, until the early morning hours. For some, "whatever" probably included visiting gambling rooms and keno parlors. For others it was an excursion to Chicago's red-light district, where, on orders from Mayor Wentworth, a police raid was conducted and a number of delegates were figuratively caught with their pants down in one of the fancier establishments.[365] Of course, the local businessmen "protested that this was no way to encourage the tourist trade."[366]

Murat Halstead, a journalist from the *Cincinnati Commercial* who was staying at the Tremont House, not only described the partying antics of the delegations generally but those of his irrepressible roommates specifically: "Many of the delegates kept up the excitement nearly all night. At two o'clock this morning part of the Missouri delegation were singing songs in the parlor. There was still a crowd of fellows caucusing—and the glasses were still clinking in the bar rooms—and far down the street a brass band was making the night musical."[367] He was wakened one morning by a vehement debate among his roommates, and rubbing his eyes, "discovered they were sitting up in bed playing cards to see who should pay for gin cock-tails *[sic]* all around, the cock-tails being an indispensable preliminary to breakfast."[368]

Butler and Delahay apprised Lincoln of what transpired on the day the convention convened. Butler wrote that Iowa, New Hampshire, and Indiana stood as a unit for him; Ohio delegates were undecided and fighting among themselves, but Lincoln would get the votes on the third ballot if he was still in the game; Massachusetts had sent for Yates and Henry S. Lane to consult with them; Butler thought Wentworth had a change of heart and was now for Lincoln; and that Lincoln's chances were good.[369]

Delahay opined if Seward did not get it done early in the balloting, Lincoln would be nominated; New Hampshire would be with Lincoln from the beginning and after a vote or two, Massachusetts and Vermont would climb on board; New York continued to send in reinforcements, and while bankers, rounders, gamblers, and blowers were thick from that city, Delahay was not discouraged and "shall never give up the Ship while a rope remains to be handled. . . ."[370]

Two events deserve special mention. On one evening the Wigwam hosted an exhibition drill of an organization called the Chicago Zouaves. The group was led by a young lawyer named Elmer Ellsworth. The Zouaves wore picturesque uniforms and drilled on the stage with military precision and discipline, performing acrobatic feats as a unit. One year and six days after the convention adjourned, the leader of the group, then Colonel Ellsworth, would be one of the first to die in the Civil War and his body would lie in state in the White House.[371]

And, on another evening during the week, if you wanted a diversion from the political gossip and the clamor of the hotels, there was a delightful comedy, *My American Cousin*, being performed at McVicker's Theater and advertised in the *Chicago Tribune* and *Chicago Times*.[372] Although it was not an award-winning play, it later became stamped in the minds of all Americans when President Abraham Lincoln went to Ford's Theatre to enjoy its presentation shortly after the Civil War came to an end. That was the night Lincoln was assassinated by John Wilkes Booth.

While most of the delegates were enjoying their outing, the candidates' campaign teams worked hard to attract additional support and to maintain what they had already reaped. The Lincoln team "ran from delegation to delegation, haranguing, pleading, promising."[373] Knowing the likelihood of getting additional bloc votes improbable, the Lincoln team concentrated on key men in each state delegation. If converted, these men "could be used as levers to pry others from their solid allegiance to some native son."[374]

On Thursday morning, May 17, 1860, with their band arrayed in its splendor, the Seward forces "made a demonstration this morning in the form of a procession. . . . [The] procession was four abreast, filing away in a cloud of dust—and one of their orators, mounted upon a door-step, with hat and cane in his hands, was haranguing them as a captain might address his soldiers marching to battle."[375] When they approached the Tremont House, where the Lincoln headquarters was set up, they proceeded to give a rousing cheer for Seward, a vocal demonstration of political might.

The convention reconvened at 10 a.m. Again the convention hall was packed and thousands were milling outside. At this session, there was a lengthy debate whether to admit the delegates from the five slave states—Kentucky, Maryland, Missouri, Texas, and Virginia—and the three territories—Kansas, Nebraska, and the District of Columbia—and, "[T]he anti-Seward men were anxious to put out Virginia and Texas, particularly Texas, fearing that those States would decide the contest in favor of Seward."[376] In the end, all delegates were seated—a win for the Seward team.

A fight also developed over the number of votes necessary for nomination. The anti-Seward faction wanted to put every obstacle possible in Seward's path to the nomination and insisted the necessary number to nominate be 304, a majority of the whole number of votes if all states of the Union were represented at the convention. The Seward men, knowing it would be impossible for Seward to garner 304 votes, vehemently insisted that only a majority of the whole number of votes in the convention should nominate—233. The Seward men won their second skirmish.[377]

At the afternoon session, the convention considered the platform. The chief goal in drafting the platform was to define the party's stand on the primary issue of the day: slavery. "All shades of opinion on the slavery question, from beliefs of the out-and-out Abolitionists to those of men who accepted the popular sovereignty theory, had to be harmonized." The result of their efforts was that the party stood opposed, not to slavery, but to slavery extension and had no "desire to interfere with slavery in its existing limits."[378] The platform that was finally adopted also "embraced the immediate admission of Kansas, free homesteads to actual settlers, river and harbor improvement of a national character, a railroad to the Pacific Ocean, and the maintenance of existing naturalization laws."[379]

Although there were no major arguments over the platform, a skirmish ensued over an amendment that would strike from the platform the opening words of the Declaration of Independence.[380] As the matter was being considered, the anti-Seward forces, knowing the next order of business was to ballot for a presidential candidate, used as much time as possible to insure there would be no vote taken on that day on the nomination. Shortly thereafter, at about 6 p.m., the matter was decided and the Seward forces had won their third skirmish.

The New Yorkers could smell blood and readied themselves for the kill. "All through the day they were in high spirits, and absolutely confident that the Convention was in their hands."[381] Weed was determined to demonstrate Seward was the strongman of the convention and had his supporters dispersed through the audience with orders to yell and shout whenever Seward's name was mentioned. After a motion to adjourn had been defeated, the New Yorkers wanted to proceed and renewed their motion to ballot for a candidate for president.[382]

More Luck for Lincoln

Again Lady Luck smiled on the Lincoln campaign. This time, it was a great big smile, a "but for" smile. Before a vote could be taken to proceed, the chairman announced that the printed list of ballots, or tally sheets, had not been delivered. At that time, an anonymous voice, a person who apparently didn't want to sit and wait or possibly an opponent of Seward, called out to adjourn until 10 a.m. on Friday.[383] A motion to adjourn is always in order and takes precedence over all other motions. After a vote, the chair declared the motion carried. The delegates adjourned.[384] The anti-Seward forces had won an important victory.

Halstead, the *Cincinnati Commercial* reporter, wrote stories on the convention in which he made three separate references to the adjournment on the second day that postponed the nomination of candidates. Halstead's first reference was succinct: "The Convention adjourned without taking a ballot for President, as the tally sheets were not prepared."[385]

In the next reference, he pointed out, "So confident were the Seward men, when the platform was adopted, of their ability to nominate their great leader, that they urged an immediate ballot and would have had it if the clerks had not reported that they were unprovided with tally sheets. The cheering of the thousands of spectators during the day, indicated that a very large share of the outside pressure was for Seward."[386]

Halstead went even further in his third reference and proffered his opinion of the significance the missing tally sheets had on the Seward campaign:

> After adjournment on Thursday (the second day), there were few men in Chicago who believed it possible to prevent the nomination of Seward. His friends had played their game to admiration, and had been victorious on every preliminary skirmish. When the platform had been adopted, inclusive of the Declaration of Independence, they felt themselves already exalted upon the pinnacle of victory. They rejoiced exceedingly, and full of confidence, cried in triumphant tone, "call the roll of states." But it was otherwise ordered. The chair announced that the tally sheets had not been prepared, and that it would subject the clerks to great inconvenience to proceed to a ballot at that time. The Seward men expressed themselves greatly disgusted and were still unwilling to adjourn. A motion was made to adjourn, however, and after an uncertain response, very little being done either way, the chair pronounced the motion for adjournment carried. The Seward men were displeased but not disheartened. They considered their hour of triumphing with brains and principle, over presumptions of expediency, as merely postponed.[387]

What a stroke of phenomenal luck for the Lincoln men! If the printer had delivered the tally sheets on time, Senator William Henry Seward would, in all likelihood, have been nominated for president.[388] At that time, the Seward campaign had everything going for it. It had the "outside pressure" (the noise) and the momentum to capture the nomination, primarily because the Seward opposition had not yet centered on a compromise candidate. Whoever the printer was, the Lincoln team should have taken him out for a beer, or better yet, a steak dinner and champagne.

Also credit should go to the unidentified individual who moved to adjourn. If there ever was a memorial for unknown political-convention soldiers, that individual would certainly be represented. Without a doubt, his four little words, "I move to adjourn," were of historic significance.

When Weed walked from the hall that afternoon, he greeted the Illinoisians cordially. He expected the showdown tomorrow and, having received pledges from Massachusetts, Michigan, Minnesota, Wisconsin, and California, Weed anticipated victory and, for the good of party unity, he again graciously proposed to put Lincoln on the ticket as vice president.[389]

Of course, this excited the Lincoln men and the proposal was relayed to Davis. Davis, who had been caucusing with New Jersey, said that Weed had made the same proposal to New Jersey with a minor modification. Weed's proposal to them was Seward for president and New Jersey's Dayton for vice president.[390]

Although the New Yorkers failed to nominate their favorite on that Thursday afternoon in Chicago, it did not stop them from celebrating. The delay was an inconvenience only. With the admission of the delegates from Virginia and Texas, they were in a "high feather"[391] and believed Seward was just hours away from being nominated for the highest office in the land. Taking the nomination for granted, Weed played host to a pre-victory champagne banquet for the delegates and 300 bottles of the bubbly cascaded down grateful throats. All night Seward bands marched about, serenading the delegations from other states. "To these revelers, the battle seemed all over but the shouting."[392]

Not only the New Yorkers but Halstead and Greeley echoed the shared belief that Seward would be nominated the next day. In fact Halstead claimed that "every one of the forty thousand men in attendance upon the Chicago Convention will testify that at midnight of Thursday . . . the universal impression was that Seward's success was certain."[393] But the adjournment was a window of opportunity that Davis and his team would use to their advantage.

Chapter 16

A Window of Opportunity

As soon as the convention adjourned for the day, Davis and his lieutenants convened a war council to review the day's activities, make plans, and pass out assignments for the next day's final assault to capture the nomination.

Earlier that day Lincoln had sent a message to his team, in response to a claim that he was as radical as Seward, and admonished them to make no deals that would bind him.[394] Davis, who had a tendency to speak his mind in a few words, after reading Lincoln's note, outdid himself and is reported to have said, "Lincoln ain't here and don't know what we have to meet!"[395] With that said, Davis proceeded with his final plans as if he had never gotten the message from Lincoln.

Davis's reaction was shared by other members of the team. They were completely focused on their goal and were determined to do what they had to do in order to get Lincoln nominated. If successful, they would worry about the fallout later. On this Thursday night, the eve of the crucial vote, the Lincoln team had more important things to consider and deal with.

Reviewing the events of the day, Davis knew defeat was at hand when the New Yorkers cried out for the vote. Some writers have suggested that Divine Providence lent a helping hand at this critical time. Regardless, Lincoln's candidacy was still alive and, to a man, the team members were tired, dog tired. But they knew there was only one more tomorrow. For a Lincoln success, it was do-or-die time.

All day Thursday the Seward supporters had led the charge, applying the outside pressure as the Seward campaign rolled on, winning skirmish after skirmish. The Seward team, headed by the prizefighter Hyer, with his merry gang of "irrepressibles," had led the convention hall cheering and yelling. As prearranged, Hyer's gang had been dispersed throughout the crowd. Every time Seward's name was mentioned, they followed orders and vigorously shouted and demonstrated.[396] To a bystander, it appeared the crowd supported Seward's candidacy and that Seward was the overwhelming choice for president.

How to repress the "irrepressible" tide was a major topic on the Lincoln war council agenda that night. The council members were of the opinion that there was a need to cut into Seward's support in the convention hall and, if at all possible, increase Lincoln's support group. The Lincoln command, being political realists, devised a plan that would accomplish both objectives and turn the tables on Seward supporters. The plan was uncomplicated in the abstract—pack the hall with an enthusiastic band of Lincoln followers and, at the same time, cut back on the number of Seward howlers—but it involved what would today be classified as a dirty trick.[397]

In addition to the tickets normally passed out to the Illinois contingent, the Lincoln team decided to mobilize another 1,000 Lincoln rooters to crowd out the Seward supporters. To insure their entry into the convention hall, Lamon and Fell supposedly had counterfeit tickets printed that night, and official signatures forged, for distribution to the newcomers, all of whom were instructed to come early to make sure they could get into the hall.[398]

This little task, getting an additional 1,000 warm bodies, was easier said than done. Remember, in 1860 there were no telephones or instant communications. To accomplish this coup required personal contact be made with the new recruits to persuade them to join the team and report early. Without a doubt, many Republicans worked frantically and diligently throughout the night recruiting the new rooters.

The Lincoln team had been in the convention hall on Wednesday and Thursday and witnessed firsthand the decisive impact that crowd noise played in convention politics. "It was evident at once that the members of the convention—some 500 out of the attendant 10,000—were not more interested in its proceedings than the spectators, whose approval and disapproval, quickly and emphatically expressed, swayed, and to a degree controlled, the delegates."[399]

The Lincoln backers' plan for Friday's finale went a step further. It added volume to numbers. Not only would they pack the galleries with additional Lincoln partisans, they persuaded two men with ear-piercing voices to join the Lincoln team. Both were "past masters of the stentorian art."[400] One was a Doctor Ames of Chicago, who "had a larynx reputedly so powerful that on a calm day he could shout across Lake Michigan!"[401] The other a man, name unknown, who lived "near Ottawa [and] who had never met his equal in long distance bellowing."[402] "These two men met some of the Illinois delegation at the Tremont House, and were instructed to organize each a body of men to cheer and shout, which they speedily did, out of the crowds which were in attendance from the Northwest."[403] They were placed on opposite sides of the convention hall and they, and all Lincoln partisans in the hall, were to cheer on signal and keep on cheering as long as they were physically able or until their lungs burst. The signal to erupt into a "spontaneous demonstration" was whenever delegate Burton Cook pulled his handkerchief out of his pocket, and to continue the demonstration until he put it back.[404] "The women present had been requested to wave their handkerchiefs at every mention of Lincoln's name. Hundreds of flags had been distributed to be used the same way."[405]

Leaving no stone unturned in applying outside pressure, "[a] series of signals had been arranged to communicate to the crowd outside the Wigwam when a roar from them might influence the convention within."[406] Davis wanted to make it appear that enthusiasm for Lincoln's nomination was all but "irrepressible," to borrow the Seward campaign catchword, and maybe it would sway a wavering delegate when the vote was taken.

Davis, Butler, and Delahay also reported in to Lincoln on May 17. Davis telegraphed that he was "very hopeful" and then cautioned

Lincoln not to be "excited."[407] Butler wrote that whole contest was between Seward and Lincoln.[408] Delahay pessimistically advanced his belief that the Lincoln team was being outgeneraled by the New Yorkers, that they had to "fight the devil with fire," and maybe make a deal or two to get the nomination.[409] And Delahay wasn't the only Lincolnite considering fighting the devil with fire.

The Lincoln team proved that, between 6 p.m. on a Thursday afternoon and 10 a.m. on Friday, a small group of determined men could move "heaven & Earth." There were late night meetings and, of course, a last effort to strike a deal. While his lieutenants were mobilizing the Lincoln ground forces for the finale and having the counterfeit tickets printed, Davis attended a caucus, "the committee of twelve," as it came to be known. This group consisted of three delegates from each of the four crucial states—Illinois, Indiana, New Jersey, and Pennsylvania—to see if they could agree on a candidate to challenge Seward.[410]

However, Davis, before going to the committee of twelve meeting, was alerted by an Indiana friend that the Bates organization was making a run at the Pennsylvania and Indiana delegations and was engaged in a consultation at the Cook County Courthouse. He dispatched Browning and Koerner to the courthouse to keep the meeting honest and spread the Lincoln message. When they arrived, the Bates spokesman was finishing his sales pitch, claiming that Bates, formerly a prominent Whig who had ties with the American Party, was the ideal candidate in the two states. Shortly, other Lincoln men arrived and the courtroom was soon crowded with Lincoln supporters.[411]

Koerner responded for Lincoln and the former Democrat claimed that even if Bates headed the ticket, he would not win his home state (Missouri) against Douglas; expressed astonishment that any German would support Bates because of his connection with the Know Nothings; and concluded that German Republicans in other states would never support Bates. Browning then took the floor. He argued that Lincoln would satisfy the Whig factions in both states,[412] and because he opposed the Know Nothings, Lincoln would get the foreign Republican vote.[413]

The two delegations each went into executive session. Indiana voted to go with Lincoln from the start. The majority of the Pennsylvania delegates wanted to go with Lincoln on the second ballot.[414] Even though they had effectively handled the Bates sortie, both Browning and Koerner were aware that the voting in a caucus is not a binding vote.

The committee of twelve caucus that Davis attended that evening was solely to discuss the likelihood of the doubtful states uniting behind a candidate who could win them. Inasmuch as a "majority of the delegates from the doubtful States were of the opinion that neither one of the States could be carried by William H. Seward if he should be nominated by the convention,"[415] the importance of this meeting cannot be overstated. Taking for granted that the states carried by Fremont in 1856 would be in the Republican fold in 1860, success in the November election required a candidate who could win the four states. If they couldn't agree, Seward would probably be nominated and the party defeated. If they could agree, their selection would have the inside track to the nomination.

But if not Seward, then who? Three of the four crucial states had favorite sons—Abraham Lincoln of Illinois, William L. Dayton of New Jersey, and Simon Cameron of Pennsylvania—and it was up to the committee to choose which man could win the four states. Davis and Judd were two members of the Illinois contingent. Judd asked the Lincoln men in the Iowa delegation to attend the caucus to add numbers to the Lincoln support roster. It also didn't hurt that Caleb Smith—now a firm Lincoln supporter, possibly with his own personal agenda to advance—headed the Indiana trio.[416]

The meeting began shortly after 6 p.m. in David Wilmot's rooms in the Tremont House.[417] Sometime around 10 p.m., Horace Greeley stuck his head in and asked if the committee had agreed on a candidate. When he was told a decision had not been made, he left and telegraphed his paper: "My conclusion from all that I can gather tonight is that opposition to Governor Seward cannot concentrate on any candidate and that he will be nominated."[418]

Noted a Davis biographer, "After Greeley had left, it was suggested that they see how many votes [from the four crucial states] each of the candidates had. When Davis showed the committee the results achieved by his workers in the past five days, it became apparent at once that Lincoln had far more votes than any candidate except Seward."[419] Before the session was over, the committee of twelve from the four doubtful states reached an agreement: "in case Lincoln's votes reached a specified number on the following day, the votes of the States represented in that meeting, so far as these 12 men could affect the result, should be given to him."[420]

The New Jersey and Pennsylvania committee members agreed to present their plan to their delegations and urge them to vote for Lincoln. Later that night the New Jersey delegation ratified the action.[421] However, there was a slight problem. Pennsylvania would not caucus until 9 a.m. on Friday, an hour before the convention was to reconvene.[422]

After the subcommittee meeting broke up sometime around 11 p.m., the hours stretching between then and sunrise were put to good use by Davis and other Lincoln supporters. In fact, "[t]here were hundreds of Pennsylvanians, Indianians, and Illinoisans, who never closed their eyes that night."[423] The Lincoln team went from delegation to delegation, spreading the good news that the battleground states of Illinois, Indiana, New Jersey, and Pennsylvania had finally agreed on a candidate who could win the four states, Abraham Lincoln, and they implored them to throw their support to Lincoln, too.[424]

The Lincoln team then unleashed a barrage of negative rumors, via a whispering campaign. The timing was perfect. There was no way the New Yorkers could effectively respond; time had simply run out. The more Weed spent trying to buy support and the more his bands and irrepressibles marched for Seward, the better Lincoln looked as the rail-splitter and man of the people. The Lincoln people spread the word Seward was the candidate of commercialism and corrupt political rule, and all the gold in the world would not help Seward carry the doubtful states.[425]

Another rumor was that neither Indiana nor Pennsylvania had ever gone Republican in a general election, nor had they elected a Republican governor. The Republican candidates for governor in those two states, in addition to the gubernatorial candidate in Illinois, threatened to drop out of the campaign if Seward was nominated.[426]

The gubernatorial candidates of Indiana and Pennsylvania, Henry Lane and Andrew Curtin, also went from caucus room to caucus room that night, spreading the same message they had in Wilmot's rooms: Seward would divide the party, whereas Lincoln would unite the party. Lane worked feverishly on the Vermont and Virginia delegations.

Finally, understanding how crucial the Pennsylvania vote was to Lincoln's chances, Davis decided to act quickly. Once they realized their man Cameron failed to generate any excitement outside of the state, the Pennsylvanians "went through the last violent throes of coming to a decision,"[427] and were ready to explore options making the state a major player in the selection of a candidate. Upon hearing Ray's report that the Pennsylvanians would "settle for a seat in the cabinet for Cameron,"[428] Davis and Ray made an early morning call on them. Davis's well-timed rendezvous was designed to bear presidential fruit and later, when Davis returned, grinning triumphantly, he proudly announced he had tied up the Pennsylvania delegation with a promise of a cabinet post to Cameron.[429] He had pulled off a coup. Now three of the four crucial states were in his pocket. Pennsylvania's votes, coming on the second ballot, should make Lincoln's nomination a near certainty.

When the despondent Greeley heard the rumblings and rumors that had been unleashed in the early morning hours, he got his second wind and, now supporting Lincoln, visited with the delegation from his home state, Vermont, and sent his private emissary, James S. Pike, to work on the Maine delegation.[430]

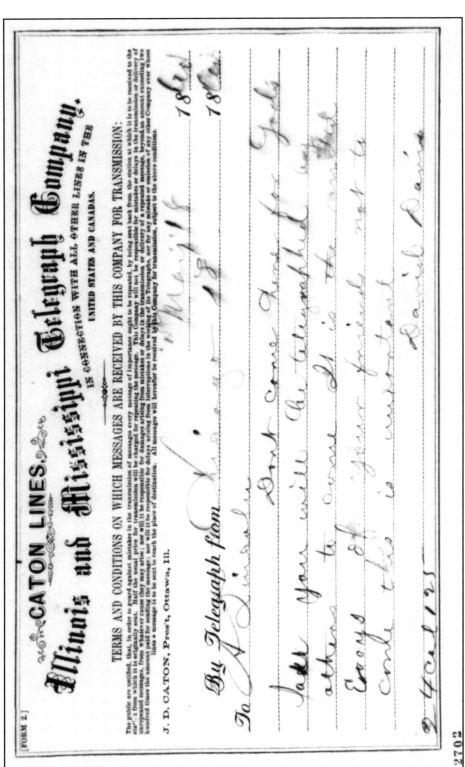

May 18 Telegram from Davis to Lincoln

Chapter 17

The Final Day

As the sun came up on Friday, May 18, 1860, Davis put his pencil to paper, and, for the last time, tallied delegate totals. Taking head counts is not an exact science, but it is a political ritual performed regularly, probably hourly. He estimated Lincoln's first ballot would reach the 100 plateau, with 48 coming from Illinois and Indiana, and the balance from friends in the Northeast, Iowa, Kentucky, Ohio, and Virginia. However, their real success would be determined only when the votes were actually cast.

Davis's counterpart, Weed, got little, if any, sleep on Thursday night. He had gotten reports throughout the night and heard the rumors that had been floated by the opposition, especially about the previous night's caucuses, but to him, the claim of Seward's inability to carry the doubtful states had become old hat. Regardless, Weed was certain he had the votes necessary to nominate Seward on the second ballot. He expected second ballot support from Pennsylvania and, coupled with the pledge he had gotten from the New Hampshire delegation at half past ten Thursday night, it should put Seward over the top.[431] "The Seward delegates, believing any concentration of the hostile forces impossible, breakfasted with triumphant faces."[432]

Seward's nomination seemed inevitable to the New Yorkers, and they prepared for his ascension to greatness by a grand parade through the Chicago streets on their way to the Wigwam. The New Yorkers' parade, about a thousand strong, was led by a marching band playing, *Oh, Isn't He a Darling*. Everybody was having a marvelous time celebrating and marching up and down the Chicago streets.

When the New Yorkers finally arrived at the Wigwam and presented their tickets, they could not get in, "although they had tickets which should have guaranteed them seats,"[433] according to one historian. Reported Halstead, "They were not where they could scream with the best effect in responding to the mention of the name of William H. Seward."[434] Instead, their places had been taken by an additional thousand Lincoln partisans who were endowed not only with "brass lungs" but with "clarion vocal powers" that were ready to be tested.[435]

For all his experience in convention politics, Weed had been blindsided by a group of amateurs. Instead of being inside cheering on their candidate as they had done on Wednesday and Thursday, many irate New York ticket-holders, now fighting mad, "had to stay outside with the milling throng, cursing their luck at being shifted off the scene of action when they were needed most."[436]

At 10 a.m. on Friday, May 18, 1860, when the gavel brought the convention to order, the crowd was charged up. The Lincoln supporters were impatiently waiting to erupt and demonstrate. The building was packed to capacity. No seat was vacant and all aisles were filled. Not another human being could be squeezed into the building.[437] Every person in the Wigwam was anxious for the spectacle of the century to begin.

The Pennsylvania delegates, having concluded their caucus, made their dramatic entry onto the platform and claimed their seats. After disposing of some minor business, the convention moved on to the nomination of candidates and, when its choice was made, a cannon that had been placed on the top of the Wigwam would be fired. A thrill went through the crowd when it saw that the tally sheets were on hand and being distributed. The unknown errant printer had finally made his delivery, and probably without his ever knowing it, the delay had a direct effect on the destiny of the country.

In 1860 there were no long nominating speeches, and the names of the several candidates were presented in a single sentence each.

Seward's name was placed in nomination first and the applause was "enthusiastic." Then Lincoln was nominated and the response was "prodigious" and clearly bested the efforts of the Seward men. Lincoln's nomination was seconded and the response surpassed "deafening" and reached "absolutely terrific." A few minutes later Seward's nomination was seconded and the shouting reached the plateau of "absolutely frantic, shrill and wild" and hundreds of spectators covered their ears in pain. Seward would have been declared the winner if the verbal war had stopped there, but the ball was back in Lincoln's court. When Lincoln's nomination was seconded the second time, the galleries exploded in a sustained frenzy of enthusiasm, according to Halstead, an "uproar was beyond description . . . a concentrated shriek that was positively awful" and accompanied it with a stomping of the feet that made the building quiver.[438]

It was a vocal show of force between the two party strongmen, pitting the candidate from the East against the candidate from the West. "[F]or a moment the struggle appeared to resolve itself into a contest of throats and lungs"[439] where "[o]ne might have supposed that the choice between them was to be governed by the volume of sound."[440] Although the Lincoln contingent, with its packed gallery, had clearly won the war of the screaming and demonstrating crowds, "the Seward men were good howlers, and the match was not far from equal."[441]

Herndon correctly sized up the coming contest: "Amid all the din and confusion, the curbstone contentions, the promiscuous wrangling of delegates, the deafening roar of the assembled hosts, the contest narrowed down to a neck-and-neck race between the brilliant statesman of Auburn and the less pretentious, but manly, rail-splitter from the Sangamon Bottoms."[442]

It was near high noon when the balloting began. The whole number of delegates was 465 with 233 needed to nominate. Soon the nation would know who, in all likelihood, would be the next president of the United States. No one, including Weed and Davis, anticipated there would be a first-round knockout delivered by any candidate. Instead, round one would be strictly a sparring round, including those candidates from favorite-son states. The round, while it would not decide the winner, would demonstrate the relative strengths and weaknesses of all candidates and identify those candidates who would answer the bell for round two.

The roll call of states proceeded in geographical order instead of alphabetical order, starting with the Northeast. Weed "counted on some solid delegations and a majority of the total vote."[443] Davis, on the other hand, believed he and his team had gotten their feet in the door in New England and cut into Seward's numbers.

The Judge was right. Maine led off in round one and of its 14 votes, Seward got 8 votes and Lincoln 6 votes. Tuck's admonition to Lincoln about latent support was proven when New Hampshire surprised the New Yorkers and broke its promise of the night before, giving Lincoln 7 votes and Seward only 1 vote. Vermont gave its 10 votes to its favorite son (Collamer) as expected; Lincoln had been promised second-round support. Massachusetts then gave Seward 21 votes and Lincoln 4; Rhode Island voted for other candidates; and Connecticut gave Lincoln 2 votes. The Northeast was not solidly for Seward as previously thought, and, out of 81 votes, Seward got 32 votes and Lincoln, 19.[444]

New York's 70 votes went to Seward amid wild applause. New Jersey was solid for its favorite son, Dayton. Pennsylvania gave most of its votes to Cameron, 4 votes went to Lincoln and 1½ votes to Seward. Maryland gave Seward 3 votes and Lincoln none. Virginia, with 23 votes, caused a stir when it gave Lincoln 14 votes and Seward 8. Kentucky also favored Lincoln over Seward—6 votes to 5. Most of Ohio's votes went to Chase but Lincoln got 8 votes as pledged. Then Indiana voted solidly for Lincoln—26 votes. Missouri voted solidly for Bates—18 votes. Michigan gave its 12 votes to Seward. Illinois voted as a unit for Lincoln, 22 votes. Iowa gave Lincoln and Seward 2 votes each. As the list of states trailed off, Seward received, as expected, solid support from Wisconsin, California, Minnesota, and Kansas, getting 32 votes and Lincoln, none.[445]

Although 12 different candidates received votes in round one, Seward clearly won the round. Seward received 173½ votes and

Lincoln was runner-up with 102 votes. The leaders far outdistanced the other major candidates: Bates, 48 votes; Cameron, 50½ votes; and Chase, 49 votes. It was clear to everyone that the contest was between Seward and Lincoln.

First Ballot Results[446]

For Mr. Seward

Maine 10	New Hampshire 1	Massachusetts......21
New York 70	Pennsylvania 1½	Maryland............ 3
Virginia 8	Kentucky................. 5	Michigan 12
Texas............. 4	Wisconsin 10	Iowa 2
California 8	Minnesota 8	Kansas 6
Nebraska 2	Dist. of Columbia.... 2	

Total 173½

For Mr. Lincoln

Maine 6	New Hampshire 7	Massachusetts...... 4
Connecticut... 2	Pennsylvania 4	Virginia 14
Kentucky....... 6	Ohio 8	Indiana................26
Illinois...........22	Iowa....................... 2	Nebraska 1

Total 102

Davis's estimate on the first ballot was just about on the money. The Lincoln plan was unfolding as if scripted and his campaign appeared about to peak. Also, Lincoln's strength on the first ballot was impressive, especially his showing in the Northeast, and should validate those promises of second-ballot support for which Davis and his team had worked so hard.

Nevertheless, Seward was the leader and was only 60 votes shy of getting the nomination. However, "the New York delegation was so thoroughly persuaded of the final success of their candidate that they did not comprehend the significance of the first ballot. Had they reflected that their delegation alone had contributed 70 votes to Seward's totals, they would have understood that outside of the Empire State, upon this first showing, Lincoln held their favorite almost to an even race."[447]

Excitement and anticipation swept over the crowd. Every person in the Wigwam realized the second ballot would be critical. The question-mark states of New Jersey, Pennsylvania and Vermont would in all likelihood determine the outcome. Weed believed if Seward and Lincoln split the vote of the favorite-son states and also-rans, Seward would win handily. Davis, on the other hand, realized if "Seward was to be beaten, it must be now"[448] and it was for the favorite-son states to say.

Round two had hardly begun when Vermont startled the crowd and gave Lincoln all 10 votes, as promised, and, a short time later, Pennsylvania, which had given Lincoln 4 votes on the first ballot and had again caucused between ballots, ignited an explosion of enthusiasm when it announced 48 votes for Lincoln. "Many delegates involuntarily rose to their feet, and cheer followed cheer. The multitude in the pit threw up their hats and canes, and hurrahed wildly. The thousands of ladies in the galleries waved their handkerchiefs, while the immense crowd outside the Wigwam screamed and shouted. For several minutes rejoicing seemed to run riot, the New York delegation, meanwhile, remaining silent in their seats."[449] Shortly, Delaware, which had given Bates 6 votes on the first ballot, also caused a minor stir when it kept its promise and gave its votes to Lincoln.

When the round was over, it was apparent the momentum had swung over to Lincoln. He clearly won round two and the two candidates were going into round three about even in delegate support. Lincoln picked up 79 additional votes on the second ballot for a total of 181 while Seward picked up 11 votes for a total of 184½. On the second ballot, Chase received 42½ votes and Bates, 35 votes.

Second Ballot Results[450]

For Mr. Seward

Maine	10	New Hampshire	1	Massachusetts	22
New York	70	New Jersey	4	Pennsylvania	2½
Maryland	3	Virginia	8	Kentucky	7
Wisconsin	10	Michigan	12	Texas	6
Minnesota	8	Iowa	2	California	8
Dist. of Columbia	2	Kansas	6	Nebraska	3

Total 184½

For Mr. Lincoln

Maine	6	New Hampshire	9	Vermont	10
Massachusetts	4	Rhode Island	3	Connecticut	4
Pennsylvania	48	Delaware	6	Virginia	14
Kentucky	9	Ohio	14	Indiana	26
Illinois	22	Iowa	5	Nebraska	1

Total 181

The Lincoln supporters began to smile; the nomination was in sight. After building momentum throughout the week, the Lincoln campaign was poised to capitalize on it when it mattered the most. It was a different story, however, for the Seward forces. Weed's worst fears were coming true before his very eyes. ". . . [T]he change in the vote of Pennsylvania, startling the vast auditorium like a clap of thunder, turned the scale"[451] and Weed had to acknowledge to himself that the nomination was slipping away.

The direction the convention was heading had to be hauntingly familiar to Weed who, in the Whig conventions of 1840 and 1848, used candidate availability—he should be acceptable to all factions—to defeat the presidential aspirations of the frontrunner, Henry Clay. "Availability, the weapon that Weed had grasped so readily in the fight against Henry Clay was more potent than all the money that New York could furnish."[452] In Chicago, at the conclusion of the second ballot, Weed faced the realization it had indeed taken a costly toll on Seward's candidacy. He could not shake the feeling, a foreboding sense of deja vu—except this time he was on the receiving end.

Surely, Weed, the political magician and kingmaker, could reach in his bag of tricks and pull out a miracle? He tried, but time was running out. He did not have the luxury of plotting his next move. In just seconds Weed had to assess Seward's waning chances and come up with a solution. The success or failure of the Seward campaign had been reduced to a single option. Weed was unhesitant and certain what he had to do: Strike a deal. To pull off the miracle, he had to look to friends past; "he needed the help of the Bates block if the tide toward Lincoln was to be stemmed. He needed Horace Greeley. Hurriedly Weed proposed a deal. But it was too late."[453] The die was cast.

As round three began, Weed could only watch and hope Seward could miraculously withstand the upcoming assault. Halstead reported, "The fate of the day was now determined. New York saw 'checkmate' [as the] next move, and sullenly proceeded with the game, assuming unconsciousness of her inevitable doom."[454]

On the third ballot, it was all but a stampede. Lincoln went on the offensive and started picking up additional votes and, to Weed's disbelief and agony, Seward began losing ground and votes. Lincoln gained 4 votes from Massachusetts, 2 from Rhode Island, 8 from New Jersey, 4 more from Pennsylvania, 9 from Maryland, 4 from Kentucky, 15 from Ohio, 4 from Oregon, ½ vote from Iowa, until his total reached 231½, just 1½ votes shy of the magic number.

It was an intense emotional moment as a hush fell over the crowd while the votes were being tallied: "The Wigwam suddenly became as still as a church, and everybody leaned forward to see whose voice would break the spell."[455] The only sounds heard were the scratching of pencils and the ticking of the telegraph instruments.

The clerks, however, weren't the only ones adding up the vote count. Many spectators, using pencils, kept the record as the vote proceeded. During this brief period, Medill, who was sitting with, and still shepherding, the Ohio delegation, quickly tallied the votes. Knowing that Ohio had a reserve of votes that had been given for Chase,[456] he looked David Cartter in the eye and offered a cabinet post for Senator Salmon Chase in return for two votes.

Then in "about 10 ticks of a watch," Cartter, an ambitious Ohio man, possibly with his own political agenda and apparently grasping that if Chase was in the cabinet there was a possibility he could land the vacant Senate seat, rose and gained recognition. "Every eye was on Cartter, and every body who understood the matter at all, knew what he was about to do." Cartter, a large man with rather striking features, spoke with a stutter. Mounting his chair, Cartter delivered the knockout punch to Seward and Weed when he announced: "I rise (eh), Mr. Chairman (eh), to announce the change of four votes of Ohio from Mr. Chase to Mr. Lincoln."[457]

Again a hush, the calm before the storm, but when the import of Cartter's actions was clear, the building shook with the cheers of the crowd. A secretary yelled out to the men stationed on the roof, "Fire the Salute! Abe Lincoln is Nominated!"[458]

Members of the Indiana delegation were hugging each other. The Illinois men all but did handstands. They had done it! This disparate group of ordinary people put aside their personal antagonisms and were made extraordinary by their commitment to their friend, Abraham Lincoln. Because of their efforts, Lincoln took a giant first step on his path to veneration and greatness.

At the convention, the Lincoln forces did not win any skirmish until they won the one that counted, and they had proved, beyond any doubt, that in politics, like horse racing, the favorite does not always win. It was a job well done.

A short time later, as Weed, left with only thoughts of what might have been if the ballots had arrived on time or if Greeley had not opposed Seward's nomination, was shedding tears, and Greeley was basking and beaming. A New York delegate reluctantly moved the nomination be made unanimous.[459]

Although crestfallen, Weed had the presence of mind to break the news to Seward. His two-word message went in this fashion:

dash /dot dot/ dash dot/ dot dot/ dot/ dot/ dot dash/ dash dot/—
spelling out L-I-N-C-O-L-N. Then this telegraphy: dash dot/ dot
dot/ dot/ dash dash/ dash dot/ dot dash/ dash/ dot/ dash dot dot—
N-O-M-I-N-A-T-E-D. Signed: dash/ dot dash dash—TW.[460]

In Auburn, the cannons went unfired and were soon hauled
away. In Springfield, the nominee, when informed of his nomination, said, "My friends, I am glad to receive your congratulations,
and as there is a little woman on Eighth Street who will be glad to
hear the news, you must excuse me until I inform her."[461]

The "Turning Point"

The delegates to the 1860 Republican Convention "had nominated
the plain, every-day, story-telling, mirth-provoking Lincoln of the
hustings" and, it "took four fearful years to give the event its true
relations and right proportions"[462]

One newspaperman who was present later aptly described
what may be the crowning significance of the 1860 Republican
Convention:

> The Chicago Convention of 1860 was much more than an organized
> body of delegates; its work much more than that of nominating
> candidates. Its transactions overshadowed in importance, outreached
> in consequences, and transcended in results those of any assembly
> of men that was ever gathered on this Continent. May 18, 1860, was
> the turning point of time.[463]

as was November 4, 2008

THE "WIGWAM" GRAND MARCH.

J.H. BUFFORD'S LITH. BOSTON.

DEDICATED TO THE

Republican Presidential Candidate.

HON. ABRM. LINCOLN.

BOSTON.
Published by OLIVER DITSON & CO. 277 Washington St.

C.C.CLAPP & CO.   BECK & LAWTON,   FIRTH POND & CO.   JOHN CHURCH JR.
Boston.   Philad ª   N.York.   Cinn.

Entered according to Act of Congress in the year 1860 by Oliver Ditson & Co in the Clerk's Office of the District Court of Mass.

Notes

Introduction A Universe in Itself

[1] Theodore H. White, *The Making of the President 1960* (New York: Barnes & Noble Books, 2004), 184.

[2] Arthur M. Schlesinger, Jr., *A Thousand Days* (Boston, MA: Houghton Mifflin Company, 1965), 28.

[3] Joseph Bucklin Bishop, *Presidential Nominations and Elections* (New York: Charles Scribner's Sons, 1916), 39.

Chapter 1 A History of Compromise

[4] "But he made up his mind as he generally did, without consultation, in the silence of his own thoughts, and once having made it up, he was inflexible." Nathaniel Wright Stephenson, *Lincoln* (Indianapolis, IN: The Bobbs-Merrill Company, 1922), 89.

[5] Wayne Whipple, *The Story-Life of Lincoln: A Biography Composed of Five Hundred True Stories Told by Abraham Lincoln and His Friends* (Philadelphia, PA: The J.C. Winston Company, Memorial Edition, 1908), 243.

[6] *United States Democratic Review* 23, 1848, "Logical Results of Republicanism," 205.

[7] William H. Herndon and Jesse W. Weik, *Herndon's Life of Lincoln* (Cleveland, OH: The World Publishing Company, 1943), 295.

Chapter 2 Lincoln's Future Opponent

[8] J.G. Holland, *The Life of Abraham Lincoln* (Springfield, MA: Gurdon Bill, 1866), 134.

[9] Ross F. Lockridge, *A. Lincoln* (Yonkers-on Hudson, NY: World Book Company, 1931), 191.

[10] Herndon and Weik, *Herndon's Life of Lincoln*, 309.

[11] In 1854, "Eli Thayer, of Massachusetts, began organizing his emigrant aid societies with intent to fill up Kansas with settlers from New England, carrying in their covered wagons, as was alleged, not only Bibles but Sharp's rifles." William Barton and William H. Townsend, *President Lincoln* (Indianapolis, IN: The Bobbs-Merrill Company, 1933), 22. See also Henry F. Graff and John A. Krout, *The Adventure of the American People: A History of the United States* (Chicago, IL: Rand McNally & Company, 1968), 262.

[12] Graff and Krout, *Adventure of the American People,* 262. Henry Ward Beecher was the brother of Harriet Beecher Stowe and it was his church in Brooklyn that invited Lincoln to speak in New York in February 1860. Lincoln's address became known as the Cooper Union Speech.

[13] Barton and Townsend, *President Lincoln,* 22–23.

[14] Graff and Krout, *Adventure of the American People*, 262.

[15] Lockridge, *A. Lincoln,* 191.

[16] Lloyd Lewis, *Chicago—The History of Its Reputation* (New York: Harcourt, Brace and Company, 1929), 88; Emmett Dedmon, *Fabulous Chicago* (New York: Random House, 1953), 51–52; Carl Sandburg, *Abraham Lincoln: The Prairie Years* (New York: Harcourt, Brace & Company, 1926), 9; and Allen Johnson, *Stephen A. Douglas: A Study in American Politics* (New York: The MacMillan Company, 1908), 259.

[17] John G. Nicolay, *A Short Life of Abraham Lincoln* (New York: The Century Co., 1903), 94.

[18] Lockridge, *A. Lincoln,* 191–192.

Chapter 3 Birth of the Republican Party

[19] One of the prime movers for a new political party was Horace Greeley, founder of the *New York Tribune* and author of editorial after editorial calling for a new organization to combat the extension of slavery.

[20] John Calvin Batchelor, *Ain't You Glad You Joined the Republicans?* (New York: Henry Holt and Company, 1996), 12.

[21] Organized in 1848, the Free Soil Party had a manifesto calling for no more slave states or slave territories.

[22] Allan Nevins. *The Emergence of Lincoln.* Vol. 2 (New York and London: Charles Scribner's Sons, 1950), 234.

[23] Arthur Meier Schlesinger, *Political and Social History of the United States, 1829–1925* (New York: The Macmillan Co., 1928), 145; Benjamin P. Thomas, *Abraham Lincoln: A Biography* (New York: Alfred A. Knopf), 1952, 145; Willard L. King, *Lincoln's Manager David Davis* (Cambridge, MA: Harvard University Press, 1960), 109.

[24] Albert E. Van Dusen, *Connecticut* (New York: Random House, 1961), 221.

[25] Van Dusen, *Connecticut,* 222.

[26] Abraham Lincoln [hereafter AL] to Elihu B. Washburne, February 9, 1855, in Roy P. Basler, editor, *The Collected Works of Lincoln* [hereafter CW], Vol. II (8 vols., New Brunswick, NJ: Rutgers University Press, 1953), 136.

[27] Nicolay, *A Short Life of Lincoln,* 100.

[28] The attack was described in "Outrage in The American Senate," Littell's *The Living Age,* Volume 50, Issue 635, July 5, 1856, 249–251, quoting an article in the June 7, 1856, *Economist.*

29 Graff and Krout, *The Adventure of the American People,* 263.

30 *Edgefield (South Carolina) Advertiser,* May 28, 1856, Secession Era Editorials Project, Department of History, Furman University.

31 Nicolay, *A Short Life of Lincoln,* 103.

32 Ibid., 75.

33 King, *Lincoln's Manager David Davis,* 127.

34 Herndon and Weik, *Herndon's Life of Lincoln,* 312.

35 Monaghan, *The Man Who Elected Lincoln,* 76, quoting John Locke Scripps of the *Chicago Democratic Press.*

36 Ibid., 76.

37 Herndon and Weik, *Herndon's Life of Lincoln,* 313.

38 Wayne Whipple, *The Story-Life of Lincoln* (Memorial Edition, 1908), 254, quoting "Lincoln's Vote for Vice-President," Jesse W. Weik. *The Century Magazine,* Vol. 76, June 1908, 186.

39 Nevins, *The Emergence of Lincoln,* 250.

40 Nicolay, *A Short Life of Lincoln,* 108–109.

41 Ibid., 109. *Obiter dictum* is a judicial decision in a matter related but not essential to a case.

Chapter 4 The Great Debates

42 Herndon and Weik, *Herndon's Life of Lincoln,* 325.

43 "Speech at Springfield, Illinois," June 16, 1854, Basler, *CW* II, 461.

44 S.A. Douglas to AL, July 30, 1858, Basler, *CW* II, 531–532.

45 William Harlan Hale, *Horace Greeley Voice of the People* (New York: Harpers & Brothers, 1950), 206.

46 Agathe Schurz, Marianne Schurz, and Carl Lincoln Schurz, editors, *The Reminiscences of Carl Schurz.* (London: John Murray, 1909), 88.

47 Because there were no large auditoriums in the West, many a political candidate delivered his speech in the open air and, if no platform was available, he made the speech while standing on a tree stump.

48 Lockridge, *A. Lincoln,* 187.

49 Schurz, *The Reminiscences of Carl Schurz,* 93.

50 Ibid., 95.

51 Ibid., 93.

52 Carl Schurz, "Abraham Lincoln," Review of 10-Volume Biography of AL by John J. Nicolay and John Hay (published in 1890), *The Atlantic Monthly,* Vol. LXVII, No. 404 (June 1891), 731.

53 Schurz, *The Reminiscences of Carl Schurz,* 90.

[54] Lockridge, *A. Lincoln,* 205.

[55] Monaghan, *The Man Who Elected Lincoln,* 118–119; John J. McPhaul, *Deadlines & Monkeyshines: The Fabled World of Chicago Journalism* (Englewood Cliffs, NJ: Prentice-Hall, Inc., 1962), 31.

[56] Noah Brooks, *Abraham Lincoln and the Downfall of American Slavery* (New York: The Lamb Publishing Company, 1888), 163.

[57] Lockridge, *A. Lincoln,* 206–207.

[58] Whipple, *The Story-Life of Lincoln,* 293.

[59] Lockridge, *A. Lincoln,* 208; Nicolay, *A Short Life of Abraham Lincoln,* 125.

[60] Whipple, *The Story-Life of Lincoln,* 293.

Chapter 5 Exploring Presidential Possibilities

[61] AL to Anson G. Henry, November 19, 1858, Basler, *CW* III, 339.

[62] Jesse Fell was the grandfather of Adlai Stevenson, the Democratic standard-bearer in 1952 and 1956.

[63] William E. Baringer, *Lincoln's Rise to Power,* (Boston, MA: Little Brown and Company, 1937), 68.

[64] Stephen B. Oates, *With Malice Toward None: The Life of Abraham Lincoln* (New York: Harper & Row, 1977), 161; and Baringer, *Lincoln's Rise to Power,* 66–68.

[65] Baringer, *Lincoln's Rise to Power,* 67.

[66] AL to Norman Judd, December 9, 1859, *The Abraham Lincoln Papers* at the Library of Congress. Transcribed and annotated by the Lincoln Studies Center, Galesburg, IL.

[67] Ibid.

[68] Baringer, *Lincoln's Rise to Power,* 68–69.

[69] Thomas J. Pickett to AL, April 13, 1859, *Lincoln Papers.*

[70] AL to Thomas J. Pickett, April 16, 1859, *Lincoln Papers.*

[71] Andrew A. Freeman, *Abraham Lincoln Goes to New York* (New York: Coward-McCann, 1960), 76–77; Ida M. Tarbell, *The Life of Abraham Lincoln* (New York: Lincoln History Society, 1903), 135.

[72] AL to Charles Ray, November 20, 1858, Basler, *CW* III, 341–342; and AL to Henry C. Whitney, November 30, 1858, Basler, *CW* III, 343.

[73] Herndon and Weik, *Herndon's Life of Lincoln,* 365.

[74] Nevins, *The Emergence of Lincoln,* 240.

[75] Nicolay, *A Short Life of Lincoln,* 130.

[76] William T. Bascom to AL, September 1, 1859, *Lincoln Papers.*

[77] Baringer, *Lincoln's Rise to Power,* 97–107.

[78] William T. Bascom to AL, October 13, 1859, *Lincoln Papers.*

[79] William O. Stoddard, *Abraham Lincoln* (New York: Frederick A. Stokes Company, 1888), 173.

[80] AL to Jesse Fell, December 20, 1859, Basler, *CW* III, 511.

[81] Ibid., 511–512.

Chapter 6 Setting the Political Stage

[82] Baringer, *Lincoln's Rise to Power,* 152.

[83] AL to Norman B. Judd, December 14, 1859, *Lincoln Papers.*

[84] Baringer, *Lincoln's Rise to Power,* 131.

[85] Tarbell, *The Life of Abraham Lincoln,* 133.

[86] Monaghan, *The Man Who Elected Lincoln,* 138.

[87] David Herbert Donald, *Lincoln* (New York: Simon & Schuster, 1995), 244.

[88] Herndon and Weik, *Herndon's Life of Lincoln,* 366–367.

[89] Barton and Townsend, *President Lincoln,* 63–64.

Chapter 7 Taking on the East

[90] James A. Briggs to AL, October 12, 1859, *Lincoln Papers.*

[91] James A. Briggs to AL, November 1, 1859, *Lincoln Papers.*

[92] Andrew A. Freeman, *Abraham Lincoln Goes to New York* (New York: Coward-McCann, 1960), 51.

[93] Charles C. Nott to AL, February 9, 1860, *Lincoln Papers.*

[94] According to Andrew Freeman, Cooper Institute is a popular name for Cooper Union.

[95] Stephen A. Douglas, "The Dividing Line Between Federal and Local Authority: Popular Sovereignty in the Territories," *Harper's New Monthly Magazine* 19 (1859), 519–537.

[96] Herndon and Weik, *Herndon's Life of Lincoln,* 368; Freeman, *Lincoln Goes to New York,* 51.

[97] Monaghan, *The Man Who Elected Lincoln,* 142.

[98] Lloyd Wendt, *Chicago Tribune: The Rise of a Great American Newspaper* (Chicago, New York, San Francisco: Rand McNally & Company, 1979), 113.

[99] Charles C. Nott to AL, February 9, 1860, *Lincoln Papers.*

[100] W.O. Stoddard, *Abraham Lincoln* (New York: Frederick A. Stokes & Brother Company, 1888), 175.

[101] Ralph G. Newman, editor, *Lincoln for the Ages* (Garden City, NY: Doubleday, 1960), 138, quoting Johnson Fairchild.

[102] "Cooper Union Speech," Basler, *CW* III, 532.

[103] Ibid., 538.

[104] Ibid., 544.

[105] Basler, *CW* III, 538.

[106] Ibid., 541.

[107] Ibid., 547.

[108] Ibid., 560.

[109] J.G. Holland, *The Life of Abraham Lincoln* (Springfield, MA: Gurdon Bill, 1866), 212.

[110] Baringer, *Lincoln's Rise to Power,* 159 and n3.

[111] Freeman, *Lincoln Goes to New York,* 86.

[112] AL to Mary Todd Lincoln, March 4, 1860, Basler, *CW* III, 555.

[113] Freeman, *Lincoln Goes to New York,* 88; William Harlan Hale, *Horace Greeley, Voice of the People* (New York: Harper & Brothers, 1950), 215.

[114] Hale, *Greeley Voice of the People,* 214–215.

[115] Herbert Mitgang, editor, *Lincoln As They Saw Him* (New York: Rinehart & Company, Inc., 1956), 158.

[116] Thomas, *Abraham Lincoln,* 205.

[117] Holland, *Life of Lincoln,* 215.

[118] Herndon and Weik, *Herndon's Life of Lincoln,* 304.

[119] Nevins, *The Emergence of Lincoln,* 242.

[120] Willard L. King, *Lincoln's Manager David Davis* (Cambridge, MA: Harvard University Press, 1960), 131.

[121] Herndon and Weik, *Herndon's Life of Lincoln,* 369.

[122] Lyman Trumbull to AL, April 24, 1860, *Lincoln Papers.*

[123] AL to Lyman Trumbull, April 19, 1860, Basler, *CW* IV, 45.

[124] James F. Babcock to AL, April 8, 1860, *Lincoln Papers.*

[125] A.S. Seaton to AL, April 24, 1860, *Lincoln Papers.*

[126] Richard M. Corwine to AL, April 30, 1860, *Lincoln Papers.*

[127] Mark W. Delahay to AL, March 26, 1860, *Lincoln Papers.*

[128] C.D. Hay to AL, March 27, 1860, *Lincoln Papers.*

[129] King, *Lincoln's Manager David Davis,* 130.

[130] Ibid.

[131] AL to Norman B. Judd, February 9, 1860, *Lincoln Papers.*

[132] Ibid.

[133] King, *Lincoln's Manager David Davis,* 131.

[134] Isaac H. Bromley, "Historic Moments: The Nomination of Lincoln," *Scribners Monthly* 14 (1893), 646.

[135] Ibid., 646.

Chapter 8 **The March Begins**

[136] Baringer, *Lincoln's Rise to Power,* 182.

[137] Holland, *The Life of Lincoln,* 42.

[138] Sandburg, *Abraham Lincoln: The Prairie Years,* 331.

[139] Barton and Townsend, *President Lincoln,* 81–82.

[140] Paul M. Angle, editor, *The Lincoln Reader* (New Brunswick, NJ: Rutgers University Press, 1947), 264.

[141] Barton and Townsend, *President Lincoln,* 81.

[142] Ibid., 82.

[143] Raymond Warren, *The Prairie President: Living Through the Years with Lincoln, 1809–1861* (Chicago, IL: The Reilly & Lee Co., 1930), 399.

[144] Thomas, *Abraham Lincoln,* 207.

[145] Francis Fisher Browne, *The Every-Day Life of Abraham Lincoln* (New York, and London, UK: G.P. Putnam's Sons, 1915), 230–231.

[146] Nevins, *The Emergence of Lincoln,* 244.

[147] Albert Shaw, *Abraham Lincoln: The Year of His Election* (New York: The Review of Reviews Corporation, 1929), 46.

[148] Angle, *The Lincoln Reader,* 265.

[149] Barton and Townsend, *President Lincoln,* 79, quoting *Life on the Circuit with Lincoln* by Henry C. Whitney, 74.

[150] Ibid., 80.

[151] Angle, *The Lincoln Reader,* 260.

[152] Orville H. Browning, *The Diary of Orville Hickman Browning.* Vol. 1: 1850–1864. Edited by Theodore C. Pease and J.G. Randall. (Springfield, IL: Illinois State Historical Library, 1925–1933), 395.

[153] Angle, *The Lincoln Reader,* 260.

[154] Sandburg, *Abraham Lincoln The Prairie Years,* 332.

[155] Baringer, *Lincoln's Rise to Power,* 58.

[156] David Davis to AL, April 23, 1860, *Lincoln Papers.*

[157] Baringer, *Lincoln's Rise to Power,* 235.

[158] Ibid., 186.

[159] Nevins, *The Emergence of Lincoln,* 246.

[160] Baringer, *Lincoln's Rise to Power,* 226.

Chapter 9 Davis Heads the Campaign

[161] Browne, *The Every-Day Life of Abraham Lincoln,* 144.

[162] David Davis to AL, November 7, 1858, *Lincoln Papers.*

[163] King, *Lincoln's Manager David Davis,* 83.

[164] Ibid.

[165] Tarbell, *The Life of Abraham Lincoln,* 144.

[166] Baringer, *Lincoln's Rise to Power,* 159. Also, Horace Greeley praised Lincoln highly for his Cooper Union speech but was not a Lincoln supporter. Greeley believed that Lincoln lacked the experience to run the government.

[167] Baringer, *Lincoln's Rise to Power,* 222.

[168] Shaw, Albert. *Abraham Lincoln: The Year of His Election* (New York: The Review of Reviews Corporation, 1929) 38 and 54.

[169] Dedmon, *Fabulous Chicago,* 55.

[170] P. Orman Ray, *The Convention That Nominated Lincoln,* 15.

[171] Bromley, "Historic Moments: The Nomination Of Lincoln," 469.

[172] Thurlow Weed Barnes, editor, *Memoir of Thurlow Weed* (Boston, MA: Houghton, Mifflin and Company, 1884), n1, 261–262.

[173] Hale, *Greeley, Voice of the People,* 209.

[174] John M. Taylor, *William Henry Seward: Lincoln's Right Hand* (New York: Harper Collins), 1991, 107.

[175] Hale, *Greeley, Voice of the People,* 209.

[176] Nevins, *The Emergence of Lincoln,* 235.

[177] Baringer, *Lincoln's Rise to Power,* 194.

[178] "Logical Results of Republicanism," 214.

[179] Nevins, *The Emergence of Lincoln,* 236.

[180] Brown, *Raymond of the Times,* 185.

[181] Nevins, *The Emergence of Lincoln,* 236.

[182] Ibid., 236.

[183] Warren, *The Prairie President,* 404.

[184] Nevins, *The Emergence of Lincoln,* 238.

[185] Oates, *With Malice Toward None,* 176.

[186] Ibid., 176–177.

[187] Wendt, *Chicago Tribune,* 121.

[188] David Davis to AL, April 23, 1860, *Lincoln Papers.*

[189] Barton, *President Lincoln,* 88.

[190] Nathaniel Wright Stephenson, *Lincoln* (Indianapolis, IN: The Bobbs-Merrill Company, 1922), 94.

[191] Richard N. Current, T. Harry Williams and Frank Freidel, *American History—A Survey* (New York: Alfred A. Knopf, 1961), 370.

Chapter 10 The Lincoln Team Gathers

[192] Tarbell, *The Life of Abraham Lincoln,* 136.

[193] The free states were Maine, New Hampshire, Vermont, Massachusetts, Rhode Island, Connecticut, New York, New Jersey, Pennsylvania, Delaware, Ohio, Indiana, Michigan, Illinois, Wisconsin, Iowa, California, Minnesota, and Oregon. The slave states were Maryland, Virginia, Kentucky, Missouri, and Texas. The territories were Kansas, Nebraska, and the District of Columbia.

[194] Shaw, *Lincoln, The Year of His Election,* 35.

[195] Baringer, *Lincoln's Rise to Power,* 216; Ray, *The Convention That Nominated Lincoln,* 11.

[196] Hale, *Greeley, Voice of the People,* 217.

[197] Monaghan, *The Man Who Elected Lincoln,* 159.

[198] Bishop, *Presidential Nominations and Elections,* 39.

[199] Nevins, *The Emergence of Lincoln,* 249.

[200] Barton and Townsend, *President Lincoln,* wrote that during the convention the rates at the larger hotels advanced to two dollars and even two and a half for room and board and since that time, "Chicago hotel-keepers have been known as shameless profiteers at the time of political conventions," 90.

[201] Murat Halstead, *Fire the Salute! Abe Lincoln is Nominated!,* edited by Paul M. Angle and Earl Schenck Miers (Kingsport, TN: Kingsport Press, Inc., 1960), 6.

[202] Bromley, "Historic Moments: The Nomination of Lincoln," 652.

[203] King, *Lincoln's Manager David Davis,* 135.

[204] Tarbell, *The Life of Abraham Lincoln,* 139.

[205] "Logan and Herndon from Springfield, Swett and Lamon from Bloomington, Samuel C. Parks from Lincoln, Moore and Weldon from Clinton, and Oliver Davis from Danville. In addition, Davis had with him Lincoln's political friends: Jesse W. Fell of Bloomington, Ozias M. Hatch, the Secretary of State, Jesse Dubois, the State Auditor, and William Butler, the State Treasurer." King, *Lincoln's Manager David Davis,* 135.

[206] Herndon and Weik, *Herndon's Life of Lincoln,* 372.

[207] Albert A. Woldman, *Lawyer Lincoln* (New York: Carroll & Graf, 1936), 101–106.

[208] Herndon and Weik, *Herndon's Life of Lincoln,* 373.

[209] Donald, *Lincoln,* 105.

[210] Sandburg, *Lincoln: The Prairie Years,* 331–332.

[211] Ibid., 70; Nicolay, *Short Life of Lincoln,* 53.

[212] Herndon and Weik, *Herndon's Life of Lincoln,* 371–372; Donald, *Lincoln,* 248.

[213] AL to Mark Delahay, March 16, 1860, Basler, *CW* IV; Herndon and Weik, *Herndon's Life of Lincoln,* 371–372.

[214] Woldman, *Lawyer Lincoln,* 102–103.

[215] Herndon and Weik, *Herndon's Life of Lincoln,* quoting Jackson Grimshaw, 366–367.

[216] Donald, *Lincoln,* 242.

[217] King, *Lincoln's Manager David Davis,* 135.

[218] Tarbell, *Life of Abraham Lincoln,* 138.

[219] Ray, *Convention That Nominated Lincoln,* 5–6; Nevins, *The Emergence of Lincoln,* 248; Barton and Townsend, *President Lincoln,* 90

[220] Dedmon, *Fabulous Chicago,* 56.

[221] Baringer, *Lincoln's Rise to Power,* 219; Tarbell, *Life of Abraham Lincoln,* 138; Hale, *Greeley, Voice of the People,* 218; and Henry B. Rankin, *Intimate Character Sketches of Abraham Lincoln* (Philadelphia and London: J.B. Lippincott Company, 1924), 197.

[222] Oates, *With Malice Toward None,* 177.

[223] Wendt, *Chicago Tribune,* 114.

[224] Baringer, *Lincoln's Rise to Power,* quoting Gustave Koerner, 231

Chapter 11 Storyline Dictates Lincoln Strategy

[225] Nicolay, *Short Life of Lincoln,* 146.

[226] Barton and Townsend, *President Lincoln,* 92.

[227] Freeman, *Lincoln Goes to New York,* 99.

[228] Oates, *With Malice Toward None,* 177–178.

[229] Baringer, *Lincoln's Rise to Power,* 172.

[230] Ibid., 227.

[231] Monaghan, *Man Who Elected Lincoln,* 161–162.

Chapter 12 The Magic Number: 233

[232] Until the convention actually met and the credentials committee determined the count of the delegates, the number of votes to nominate could not be determined. However, campaign managers worked on the assumption there would be about 475 delegates to the convention.

[233] Baringer, *Lincoln's Rise to Power,* 207.

[234] Ibid.

[235] Although Ohio was a divided delegation, Senator Chase was expected to get most of Ohio's votes on the first ballot.

[236] Baringer, *Lincoln's Rise to Power,* 207.

[237] Oates, *With Malice Toward None,* 177.

[238] AL to Samuel Galloway, March 24, 1860, *Lincoln Papers.*

[239] King, *Lincoln's Manager David Davis,* 136.

[240] Ibid., 135–136.

[241] Wendt, *Chicago Tribune,* 120.

[242] King, *Lincoln's Manager David Davis,* 136.

[243] Ibid.

[244] The shepherds performed their tasks well. First ballots totals for Lincoln from Vermont, Maine, Ohio, Kentucky, and Indiana were 46; Lincoln's second ballot totals from those five states increased to 65. Halstead, *Fire the Salute!* 39 and 41.

[245] King, *Lincoln's Manager David Davis,* 136.

[246] Ibid.

[247] Nevins, *The Emergence of Lincoln,* 249.

[248] King, *Lincoln's Manager David Davis,* 136.

[249] Ibid.

[250] Ibid.,138.

[251] Charles Roll, "Indiana's Part in the Nomination of Abraham Lincoln for President in 1860," *Indiana Magazine of History,* Volume XXV, March 1929, 4.

[252] Baringer, *Lincoln's Rise to Power,* 178.

[253] AL to Cyrus M. Allen, May 1, 1860, Basler, *CW* IV, 46–47.

[254] Baringer, *Lincoln's Rise to Power,* 214; Monaghan, *Man Who Elected Lincoln,* 162. However, the renowned Lincoln biographer, David Herbert Donald, maintains there is no foundation to the charge that Judge Davis promised a cabinet post to Caleb Smith to secure the vote of the Indiana delegation. Donald, *Lincoln,* 249.

[255] Baringer, *Lincoln's Rise to Power,* 214.

[256] Jesse K. Dubois to AL, May 13, 1860, *Lincoln Papers.*

[257] Baringer, *Lincoln's Rise to Power.* 215.

[258] Halstead, *Fire the Salute!* 38–39.

[259] Baringer, *Lincoln's Rise to Power,* 224.

[260] Bromley, "Historic Moments: Nomination of Lincoln," 650–651.

[261] Roll, "Indiana's Part in the Nomination," 3.

[262] Charles H. Ray to AL, May 14, 1860, *Lincoln Papers.*

263 William Butler to AL, May 14, 1860, (two letters), *Lincoln Papers.*

264 Mark W. Delahay to AL, May 14, 1860, *Lincoln Papers.*

265 Nathan M. Knapp to AL, May 14, 1860, *Lincoln Papers.*

266 Tarbell, *The Life of Abraham Lincoln,*144.

267 Amos Tuck to AL, May 14, 1860, *Lincoln Papers.*

268 Taylor, *William Henry Seward,* 6.

269 Thomas H. Dudley, "Memoranda on the Life of Lincoln: Lincoln's Nomination." *The Century* 40, No. 3 (1890), 478.

270 King, *Lincoln's Manager David Davis,* 134.

271 Baringer, *Lincoln's Rise to Power,* 232.

272 On the first ballot, Lincoln received 13 first ballot votes from Maine and New Hampshire to Seward's 11 votes. On the second ballot, Lincoln gained two votes; Seward's totals remained the same, 11. Halstead, *Fire the Salute!* 39 and 41.

273 Orville H. Browning, *Browning Diary,* 406–407.

274 Baringer, *Lincoln's Rise to Power,* 233.

275 Jesse K. Dubois and David Davis to AL, May 15, 1860, *Lincoln Papers.* "Old fogy politicians" probably referred to the two oldest candidates, Edward Bates and John McLean.

276 Jesse K. Dubois to AL, May 15, 1860, *Lincoln Papers.*

277 William Butler to AL, May 15, 1860, *Lincoln Papers.*

278 Mark Delahay to AL, May 15, 1860, *Lincoln Papers.*

279 Baringer, *Lincoln's Rise to Power,* 235.

Chapter 13 Second and Third Ballot Support

280 Baringer, *Lincoln's Rise to Power,* 237.

281 Ibid.

282 Tarbell, *The Life of Abraham Lincoln,* 144–145.

283 Halstead, *Fire the Salute!* iii.

284 Jesse Dubois to AL, May 13, 1860, *Lincoln Letters.*

285 Baringer, *Lincoln's Rise to Power,* 201.

286 Sam Galloway to AL, March 15, 1860, *Lincoln Letters.*

287 Baringer, *Lincoln's Rise to Power,* 237.

288 Ibid., 216–217.

289 Ibid., quoting Leonard Swett, 233.

290 Most of the Virginia delegates came from that part of Virginia that later became West Virginia. Halstead, *Fire the Salute!* 58.

291 Whipple, *Story-Life of Lincoln,* 317.

292 Baringer, *Lincoln's Rise to Power,* 252.

293 Ibid.

294 Mitgang, *Lincoln As They Saw Him,* 164–167.

Chapter 14 Thurlow Weed Heads the Seward Team

295 Baringer, *Lincoln's Rise to Power,* 295; Henry Luther Stoddard, *Horace Greeley—Printer, Editor, Crusader* (New York: G.P. Putnam's Sons, 1946), 196.

296 H.L. Stoddard, *Horace Greeley,* 196.

297 Baringer, *Lincoln's Rise to Power,* 213; Albert Shaw, *Abraham Lincoln: The Year of His Election* (New York: The Review of Reviews Corporation), 1929, 52.

298 Hale, *Greeley, Voice of the People,* 218.

299 H.L. Stoddard, *Horace Greeley,* 196.

300 Baringer, *Lincoln's Rise to Power,* 222.

301 Ibid., 222–223.

302 H.L. Stoddard, *Horace Greeley,* 199.

303 Glyndon G. Van Deusen, *Thurlow Weed: Wizard of the Lobby* (Boston, MA: Little, Brown and Company, 1947), 251–252; H.L. Stoddard, *Horace Greeley,* 197; Baringer, *Lincoln's Rise to Power,* 272–273.

304 Taylor, *William Henry Seward,* 6; Baringer, *Lincoln's Rise to Power,* 272–273.

305 Baringer, *Lincoln's Rise to Power,* 237.

306 Ibid., 238.

307 Ibid., 237.

308 Ibid., 235.

309 "[Y]ears later Cameron was reported to have said that if Weed had gone to Chicago by way of Harrisburg, Seward would have been nominated." Van Deusen, *Thurlow Weed,* 248–249.

310 Van Deusen, *Thurlow Weed,* 249.

311 Ibid., 251.

312 Barnes, *Memoir of Thurlow Weed,* 268.

313 Baringer, *Lincoln's Rise to Power,* 219.

314 Bromley, "Historic Moments: The Nomination of Lincoln," 649.

315 Tarbell, *The Life of Abraham Lincoln,* 137.

316 Halstead, *Fire the Salute!* 10–11; Van Deusen, *Thurlow Weed,* 251.

317 Halstead, *Fire the Salute!* 4.

318 Barton and Townsend, *President Lincoln,* 88.

319 Nevins, *The Emergence of Lincoln,* 249.

320 Tarbell, *The Life of Abraham Lincoln,* 138.

321 Schurz, *Reminiscences of Carl Schurz,* 176.

322 Ibid.

323 Ibid., 177.

324 "There was no disposition to enforce the strictness as to credentials from the Northern States, though a question was raised as to the admission of delegates, not well accredited, from Southern States where there was notoriously no Republican organization." Bromley, "Historic Moments: Nomination of Lincoln," 650.

325 Shaw, *Lincoln, Year of His Election,* 58.

326 Andrew A. Freeman, *Lincoln Goes to New York* (New York: Coward-McMann, Inc., 1960), 70.

327 Ibid.

328 Barton, *President Lincoln,* 89.

329 Tarbell, *Life of Lincoln,* 141.

330 Barton and Townsend, *President Lincoln,* 89. Greeley was not the only outsider who represented Oregon. The abolitionist, Eli Thayer, from Massachusetts, was also named as a delegate from Oregon. According to Bromley, Thayer was an eccentric politician "who, accepting the doctrine of popular sovereignty, had taken practical steps toward beating the slave-holders at their own game, by organizing Emigrant Aid Societies to colonize Kansas with Free-State settlers. He is not much remembered now, but the enterprises he originated saved Kansas from slavery, by filling the Territory with a majority of antislavery settlers." Bromley, "Historic Moments," 649.

331 Halstead, *Fire the Salute!* 12.

332 Hale, *Greeley, Voice of the People,* 217.

333 Barnes, *Memoir of Thurlow Weed,* 268.

334 Bromley, "Historic Moments," 649.

335 Baringer, *Lincoln's Rise to Power,* 224.

336 Barnes, *Memoir of Thurlow Weed,* 269.

337 Hale, *Greeley, Voice of the People,* 219.

338 Monaghan, *Man Who Elected Lincoln,* 160.

339 Tarbell, *Life of Lincoln,* 138.

340 Hale, *Greeley, Voice of the People,* 209.

341 Ibid., 219–220; Baringer, *Emergence of Lincoln,* 220 and 224.

342 Tarbell, *Life of Lincoln,* 139; Monaghan, *Man Who Elected Lincoln,* 160–161.

Chapter 15 The Call to Order

343 Ray, *Convention That Nominated Lincoln,* 19; Bromley, "Historic Moments," 647.

[344] Bromley, "Historic Moments," 647.

[345] Ray, *Convention That Nominated Lincoln*, 7.

[346] Ibid., 15.

[347] Bromley, "Historic Moments," 648.

[348] Ray, *Convention That Nominated Lincoln*, 8.

[349] Ibid., 16.

[350] Halstead, *Fire the Salute!* 13.

[351] Bromley, "Historic Moments," 648.

[352] Ibid., 647.

[353] Halstead, *Fire the Salute!* 13; Ray, *Convention That Nominated Lincoln*, 16–17.

[354] Halstead, *Fire the Salute!* 13.

[355] Tarbell, *Life of Lincoln*, 143; Ray, *Convention That Nominated Lincoln*, 17–18.

[356] Tarbell, *Life of Lincoln*, 143.

[357] Baringer, *Lincoln's Rise to Power*, 231.

[358] Wendt, *Chicago Tribune*, 121.

[359] Ibid.; King, *Lincoln's Manager David Davis*, 139.

[360] Bromley described Ashmun as "a handsome man of dignified presence and winning manners." He had been in the Whig Party, had served in Congress and been an intimate of Daniel Webster. Although he had been practically out of politics since 1852, he rejoined the fight against slavery. Bromley, "Historic Moments," 651.

[361] Baringer, *Lincoln's Rise to Power*, 251.

[362] Halstead, *Fire the Salute!* 10.

[363] Tarbell, *Life of Lincoln*, 143.

[364] Ray, *The Convention That Nominated Lincoln*, 21.

[365] Hale, *Greeley, Voice of the People*, 218.

[366] McPhaul, *Deadlines & Monkeyshines*, 33.

[367] Halstead, *Fire the Salute!* 15.

[368] Ibid., 7.

[369] William Butler to AL, May 16, 1860, *Lincoln Papers*.

[370] Mark W. Delahay to AL, May 16, 1860, *Lincoln Papers*.

[371] Bromley, "Historic Moments," 648.

[372] William H. Provis, Jr.; Joseph Grod; and James Stewart, compilers, *Chicago at the Time: Political Conventions in 1860, 1864, and 1868* (Chicago, IL, Harold Washington Library Center: 1996), 1.

[373] Tarbell, *Life of Lincoln*, 144.

[374] Monaghan, *Man Who Elected Lincoln*, 162.

[375] Halstead, *Fire the Salute!* 15.

[376] Ibid., 17.

[377] Halstead, *Fire the Salute!* 16–20; Bromley, "Historic Moments," 652.

[378] Bromley, "Historic Moments," 652.

[379] Nicolay, *Short Life of Lincoln,* 148.

[380] Bromley, "Historic Moments," 652–653; Nicolay, *Short Life of Lincoln,* 148.

[381] Bromley, "Historic Moments," 652.

[382] Halstead, *Fire the Salute!* 31.

[383] Barton and Townsend, *President Lincoln,* 93; Ray, *Convention That Nominated Lincoln,* 25.

[384] Baringer, *Lincoln's Rise to Power,* 263.

[385] Halstead, *Fire the Salute!* 28.

[386] Ibid., 29.

[387] Ibid., 31.

[388] Barton and Townsend, *President Lincoln,* 93 ("[I]f he [the printer] had done his work on time, William H. Seward would have been nominated."); Tarbell, *Life of Lincoln,* 145 ("[I]f the ballot had been taken on the afternoon of that day, as was at first intended, Seward would probably have been nominated."); and Ray, *Convention That Nominated Lincoln,* 25 ("[T]here is little doubt that Seward would have been nominated that night.").

[389] Monaghan, *Man Who Elected Lincoln,* 166.

[390] Ibid.

[391] Bromley, "Historic Moments," 654.

[392] Ray, *Convention That Nominated Lincoln,* 26.

[393] Halstead, *Fire the Salute!* 32.

Chapter 16 A Window of Opportunity

[394] Barton and Townsend, *President Lincoln,* 87; and Baringer, *Lincoln's Rise to Power,* 266.

[395] Wendt, *Chicago Tribune,* 121.

[396] Tarbell, *Life of Lincoln,* 137–138.

[397] Baringer, *Lincoln's Rise to Power,* 267.

[398] Ibid.

[399] Tarbell, *Life of Lincoln,* 143–144.

[400] Baringer, *Lincoln's Rise to Power,* 267.

[401] Ibid.

[402] Ibid., 268.

[403] Browne, *Every-Day Life of Lincoln,* 233.

[404] Baringer, *Lincoln's Rise to Power,* 278–279.

[405] Tarbell, *Life of Lincoln,* 148.

[406] Ibid., 148.

[407] David Davis to AL, May 17, 1860, *Lincoln Papers.*

[408] William Butler to AL, May 17, 1860, *Lincoln Papers.*

[409] Mark W. Delahay to AL, May 17, 1860, *Lincoln Papers.*

[410] Dudley, "Memoranda on Life of Lincoln," 478.

[411] Baringer, *Lincoln's Rise to Power,* 269.

[412] Ibid.; Roll, "Indiana's Part in the Nomination," 7–8.

[413] Author's note: In my research I did not find where Lincoln ever publicly opposed the Know Nothings; Browning's claim was purely convention rhetoric.

[414] Baringer, *Lincoln's Rise to Power,* 269.

[415] Dudley, "Memoranda on Life of Lincoln," 477.

[416] Baringer, *Lincoln's Rise to Power,* 270.

[417] Dudley, "Memoranda on Life of Lincoln," 478.

[418] Hale, *Greeley, Voice of the People,* 222.

[419] King, *Lincoln's Manager David Davis,* 140.

[420] Tarbell, *The Life of Abraham Lincoln,* 147.

[421] Dudley, "Memoranda on Life of Lincoln," 478; King, *Lincoln's Manager David Davis,* 140.

[422] Baringer, *Lincoln's Rise to Power,* 271.

[423] Halstead, *Fire the Salute!* 32.

[424] Baringer, *Lincoln's Rise to Power,* 272.

[425] Ibid., 273.

[426] Halstead, *Fire the Salute!* 34.

[427] Tarbell, *Life of Lincoln,* 146.

[428] Monaghan, *Man Who Elected Lincoln,* 168.

[429] Wendt, *Chicago Tribune,* 121; Nevins, *Emergence of Lincoln,* 257; Monaghan, *Man Who Elected Lincoln,* 168–169.

[430] Hale, *Greeley, Voice of the People,* 222.

Chapter 17 The Final Day

[431] Van Deusen, *Weed: Wizard of the Lobby,* 251.

[432] Nevins, *Emergence of Lincoln,* 255.

[433] Barton and Townsend, *President Lincoln,* 94.

[434] Halstead, *Fire the Salute!* 35.

[435] Ray, *Convention That Nominated Lincoln,* 21.

[436] Baringer, *Lincoln's Rise to Power,* 278.

[437] Ray, *Convention That Nominated Lincoln,* 21.

[438] Halstead, *Fire the Salute!* 37.

[439] John G. Nicolay and John Hay, "Lincoln's Nomination and Election," *The Century,* vol. 34, issue 5 (September 1887), 669.

[440] Bromley, "Historic Moments," 654.

[441] Ibid.

[442] Herndon and Weik, *Herndon's Life of Lincoln,* 373.

[443] Bromley, "Historic Moments," 654.

[444] Halstead, *Fire the Salute!* 38.

[445] Ibid., 38–39.

[446] Ibid., 39.

[447] Nicolay, *Short Life of Lincoln,* 150.

[448] Tarbell, *Life of Lincoln,* 149.

[449] Frank B. Carpenter, "How Lincoln Was Nominated." *The Century* 24, #6, (1882), 858.

[450] Halstead, *Fire the Salute!* 41.

[451] Barnes, *Memoir of Thurlow Weed,* 264.

[452] Van Deusen, *Thurlow Weed: Wizard of the Lobby,* 252.

[453] Ibid., 253; Greeley, *Voice of the People,* 223.

[454] Halstead, *Fire the Salute!* 40.

[455] Nicolay, *Short Life of Abraham Lincoln,* 151.

[456] Halstead, *Fire the Salute!* 43.

[457] Ibid., 43–44.

[458] Ibid.

[459] Baringer, *Lincoln's Rise to Power,* 291.

[460] Earl Conrad, *Man Who Would Be President* (New York: Paperback Library, Inc., 1960), 376.

[461] Tarbell, *Life of Lincoln,* 152.

[462] Bromley, "Historic Moments," 656.

[463] Ibid., 645.

Acknowledgments

Because Lincoln's first nomination in 1860 was certainly a key moment in American history, I was determined to find out the story behind his success. My research and writing of this book extended over many years and many people have helped me. My goal was to write a historical vignette that reads like a novel. There are a few works I found that stand out over all the rest: Basinger's book, Murat Halstead's account of the 1860 Republican Convention, and Isaac Bromley's article in the November 1893 issue of *Scribner's*. I also learned that the Internet is truly an information highway when I clicked on Cornell University's "Making of America" and the Lincoln Papers in the Library of Congress.

When I finally began to put pen to paper, I asked my wife, Andrea, to read and critique my early efforts. She encouraged me and has supported all my efforts, reading revision after revision, offering constructive comments. I then asked my sister, Rachel Hollis, to read and review my work. She did and, being an "old" schoolteacher, she had plenty to say.

My work progressed to the point where I had to have an outsider read it so I sent it to a book doctor—Robin Smith. She was wonderful and her suggestions were implemented. Then I asked others to read my manuscript. These individuals included family members—my brother, Neil Miner; my children, Audrey Seiter and Cathy Davis; my niece and her husband, Hack and Jeannie Wall; niece Tracy Hollis and nephew Chris Hollis—and friends—Judge John J. McGrath, Jr., Judge John Paul, Susan and Ronnie Derrow, Robert Hahn, Tony Bailey, David Ledbetter, Scott Baker, Tim Weaver, John Ellege, William Stables, Thomas Hauge, William Wentz, and Dan and Carole Duckworth.

When the work was substantially completed, I realized, to establish my Lincoln *bona fides*, I needed to have a Lincoln expert read and review my work. That expert was close at hand. Dr. Phillip Stone, president of Bridgewater College, is also the president of the Lincoln Society of Virginia. As a member of the society I wrote and informed him I had substantially completed a work on Lincoln's first nomination and asked for an appointment. To maximize my visit, I sent him a copy of the manuscript. When I arrived for the appointment it went far better than I expected. Not only had Dr. Stone read my work, he liked it!

Armed with Dr. Stone's encouragement, I began looking for a publisher, one willing to take a chance on an unknown author lacking the academic/published historian credentials demanded by mainstream publishers. Thanks to a chance reading of the *Washington Post* and seeing an advertisement wanting historical manuscripts, I sent a copy to Paula Elsey, History4All, Inc., and got a positive response. She took up the challenge to publish the manuscript and assigned Marion Meany to edit the manuscript. These two women are no-nonsense and it has been a privilege to be associated with them. Even though the outcome of the 1860 Republican Convention is known to all, I believe we have captured the energy and atmosphere of the convention so that the reader feels in the moment, captivated by the drama unfolding and unflaggingly interested in what is going on.

Enjoy and if you would like to comment, my e-mail address is jaymineratty@aol.com.

Bibliography

The Abraham Lincoln Papers at the Library of Congress. Transcribed and Annotated by The Lincoln Studies Center. Galesburg, IL.

Angle, Paul M., editor. *The Lincoln Reader.* New Brunswick, NJ: Rutgers University Press, 1947.

"An Appeal to the Free Soil Party." *The United States Democratic Review* 23, No. 125 (1848): 400.

Baringer, William E. *Lincoln's Rise to Power.* Boston, MA: Little Brown and Company, 1937.

Barnes, Thurlow Weed, editor. *Memoir of Thurlow Weed.* Boston, MA: Houghton, Mifflin and Company, 1884.

Barton, William E., and William H. Townsend. *President Lincoln.* Vol. 1. Indianapolis, IN: The Bobbs-Merrill Company, 1933.

Basler, Roy P., editor. *The Collected Works of Lincoln.* 8 vols. New Brunswick, NJ: Rutgers University Press, 1953.

Batchelor, John Calvin. *Ain't You Glad You Joined the Republicans? A Short History of the GOP.* New York: Henry Holt and Company, 1996.

Bates, David Homer. *Lincoln in the Telegraph Office: Recollections of the United States Military Telegraph Corps During the Civil War.* New York and London, UK: D. Appleton-Century Company, 1939.

Bishop, Joseph Bucklin. *Presidential Nominations and Elections.* New York: Charles Scribner's Sons, 1916.

Bromley, Isaac H. "Historic Moments: The Nomination of Lincoln." *Scribners Monthly* 14 (1893): 645–656.

Brooks, Noah. *Abraham Lincoln and the Downfall of American Slavery.* New York: The Lamb Publishing Company, 1898.

Brown, Francis. *Raymond of the Times.* New York: W.W. Norton and Company, 1951.

Browne, Francis F. *The Every-Day Life of Abraham Lincoln: A Narrative and Descriptive Biography with Pen-pictures and Personal Recollections by Those Who Knew Him.* New York and London, UK: G.B. Putnam's Sons, 1915.

Browning, Orville H. *The Diary of Orville Hickman Browning.* Vol. 1: 1850–1864. Edited by Theodore C. Pease and J. G. Randall. Springfield, IL: Illinois State Historical Library, 1925–1933.

Carpenter, Frank B. "How Lincoln Was Nominated." *The Century* 24, #6, (October 1882): 853–859.

Conrad, Earl. *The Man Who Would Be President.* New York: Paperback Library, Inc., 1961. By arrangement with G. Putnam's Sons.

Current, Richard N., T. Harry Williams, and Frank Freidel. *American History—A Survey.* New York: Alfred A. Knopf, 1961.

Dedmon, Emmett. *Fabulous Chicago.* New York: Random House, 1953.

Donald, David Herbert. *Lincoln.* New York: Simon & Schuster, 1995.

Douglas, Stephen A. "The Dividing Line Between Federal and Local Authority: Popular Sovereignty in the Territories." *Harper's New Monthly Magazine* 19 (1859): 519–537.

Dudley, Thomas H. "Memoranda on the Life of Lincoln: Lincoln's Nomination." *The Century* 40, No. 3 (1890): 477–479.

Goodwin, Doris Kearns. *Team of Rivals: The Political Genius of Abraham Lincoln.* New York: Simon & Schuster, 2005.

Freeman, Andrew A. *Abraham Lincoln Goes to New York.* New York: Coward-McCann, 1960.

Graff, Henry F. and John A. Krout. *The Adventure of the American People: A History of the United States.* Chicago, IL: Rand McNally & Company, 1968.

Green, Israel. "The Capture of John Brown." *The North American Review* 141 (1885): 564–569.

Hale, William Harlan. *Horace Greeley, Voice of the People.* New York: Harper & Brothers, 1950.

Halstead, Murat. *Fire the Salute! Abe Lincoln is Nominated!* Edited by Paul M. Angle and Earl Schenck Miers. Kingsport, TN: Kingsport Press, Inc., 1960.

Herndon, William H., and Jesse W.Weik. *Herndon's Life of Lincoln.* Cleveland, OH: The World Publishing Company, 1943.

Holland, J.G. *The Life of Abraham Lincoln.* Springfield, MA: Gurdon Bill, 1866.

Johnson, Allen. *Stephen A. Douglas: A Study in American Politics.* New York: The MacMillan Company, 1908.

King, Willard L. *Lincoln's Manager David Davis.* Cambridge, MA: Harvard University Press, 1960.

Lewis, Lloyd. *Chicago: The History of Its Reputation.* New York: Harcourt, Brace & Company, 1929.

Lockridge, Ross F. *A. Lincoln.* Yonkers-on Hudson, NY: World Book Company, 1931.

"Logical Results of Republicanism." *The United States Democratic Review* 43 (October 1859): 201–215.

MacPhaul, John J. *Deadlines & Monkeyshines: The Fabled World of Chicago Journalism.* Englewood Cliffs, NJ: Prentice-Hall, Inc., 1962.

Mitgang, Herbert, editor. *Lincoln As They Saw Him.* New York: Rinehart & Company, Inc., 1956.

Monaghan, Jay. *The Man Who Elected Lincoln.* Indianapolis, IN, and New York: Bobbs-Merrill Company, 1956.

Nevins, Allan. *The Emergence of Lincoln.* Vol. 2. New York and London, UK: Charles Scribner's Sons, 1950.

Newman, Ralph G., editor. *Lincoln for the Ages.* Garden City, NY: Doubleday, 1960.

Nicolay, John G. *A Short Life of Abraham Lincoln.* New York: The Century Co., 1903.

Nicolay, John G., and John Hay. "Lincoln's Nomination and Election." *The Century* 34, No. 5 (September1887): 658–685.

Oates, Stephen B. *With Malice Toward None: The Life of Abraham Lincoln.* New York: Harper & Row, 1977.

Oldroyd, Osborn H. *Lincoln's Campaign or The Political Revolution of 1860.* Chicago, IL: Laird & Lee, 1896.

"Outrage in the American Senate." Littell's *The Living Age,* New York, Vol. 50, No. 635, July 5, 1856: 249–251.

Provis, William H., Jr., Joseph Grod, and James Stewart, compilers. *Chicago at the Time: Political Conventions in 1860, 1864, and 1868.* Chicago, IL, Harold Washington Library Center, 1996.

Rankin, Henry B. *Intimate Character Sketches of Abraham Lincoln.* Philadelphia, PA and London, UK: J.B. Lippincott Company, 1924.

Ray, P. Orman. *The Convention That Nominated Lincoln: An Address Delivered Before the Chicago Historical Society on May 18, 1916, the Fifty-Sixth Anniversary of Lincoln's Nomination for the Presidency.* Chicago, IL: The University of Chicago Press, 1916.

Roll, Charles. "Indiana's Part in the Nomination of Abraham Lincoln for President in 1860." *Indiana Magazine of History* 25, No. 1 (March 1929):1–13.

Sandburg, Carl. *Abraham Lincoln: The Prairie Years.* New York: Harcourt, Brace & Company, 1926.

Schlesinger, Arthur Meier. *Political and Social History of the United States, 1829–1925.* New York: The Macmillan Co., 1928.

Schlesinger, Jr., Arthur M. *A Thousand Days: John F. Kennedy in the White House.* Boston, MA: Houghton Mifflin Company, 1965.

Schurz, Agathe, Marianne Schurz, and Carl Lincoln Schurz, editors. *The Reminiscences of Carl Schurz.* London, UK: John Murray, 1909.

Shaw, Albert. *Abraham Lincoln: The Year of His Election.* New York: The Review of Reviews Corporation, 1929.

Stephenson, Nathaniel W. *Lincoln: An Account of His Personal Life, Especially of its Springs of Action as Revealed and Deepened by the Ordeal of War.* Indianapolis, IN: The Bobbs-Merrill Company, 1922.

Stoddard, Henry L. *Horace Greeley: Printer, Editor, Crusader.* New York: G.P. Putnam's Sons, 1946.

Stoddard, William O. *Abraham Lincoln.* New York: Frederick A. Stokes & Brother Company, 1888.

Tarbell, Ida M. *The Life of Abraham Lincoln.* New York: Lincoln History Society, 1903.

Taylor, John M. *William Henry Seward: Lincoln's Right Hand.* New York: Harper Collins, 1991.

Thomas, Benjamin P. *Abraham Lincoln: A Biography.* New York: Alfred A. Knopf, 1952.

Van Deusen, Glyndon G. *Thurlow Weed: Wizard of the Lobby.* Boston, MA: Little, Brown and Company, 1947.

Van Dusen, Albert E. *Connecticut.* New York: Random House, 1961.

Warren, Raymond. *The Prairie President: Living Through the Years with Lincoln, 1809–1861.* Chicago, IL: The Reilly & Lee Co., 1930.

Wendt, Lloyd. *Chicago Tribune: The Rise of a Great American Newspaper.* Chicago, IL; New York; San Francisco, CA: Rand McNally & Company, 1979.

Whipple, Wayne. *The Story-Life of Lincoln: A Biography Composed of Five Hundred True Stories Told by Abraham Lincoln and His Friends.* Philadelphia, PA: The J.C. Winston Company, Memorial Edition, 1908.

White, Theodore H. *The Making of the President 1960.* New York: Barnes & Noble Books, 2004. Originally published by Atheneum, 1961.

Whitney, Henry C. *Lincoln the Citizen.* New York: Baker & Taylor Co., 1908.

Wilkinson, William C. "Daniel Webster and the Compromise of 1850." *Scribners Monthly* 12 (1876): 412.

Woldman, Albert A., *Lawyer Lincoln.* New York: Carroll & Graf, 1936.

Illustration Credits

Index

About the Author

J ay C. Miner was born in Clewiston, Florida, on December 25, 1938, where he spent his childhood and early life. After attending Florida State University, he joined the U.S. Army and saw extended service when the Berlin Wall was being built. In 1963 he relocated to Washington, DC, where he attended American University and served as a U.S. Capitol policeman. During this time he not only worked the Kennedy funeral but he also was a witness to numerous Congressional hearings on the Ku Klux Klan and Students for a Democratic Society.

After he graduated from American University with a degree in government, he attended the Walter F. George School of Law, Mercer University, in Macon, GA, where he was a member of the Law Review and published twice. Receiving his Juris Doctor degree in 1969, he returned to Washington and worked for the Interstate Commerce Commission as an attorney adviser.

In 1976, he left the Washington area and subsequently opened a private law practice in the Ozarks, specializing in criminal and municipal law, and served as a city attorney for over 20 years. During those years he became involved in politics, both as a candidate and campaign worker. He also pursued his fascination with the first nomination of Abraham Lincoln. He has many Lincoln works in his library, starting with J.G. Holland's *The Life of Abraham Lincoln,* published in 1865. Using these works as a foundation, he expanded his search to include biographies on the movers and shakers of 1860, correspondence between Lincoln and his friends, and articles published in the leading journals of the time. His search has culminated in the creation of a dramatic account of Lincoln's first nomination—factually accurate and richly detailed—and has provided an invaluable snapshot of a very important event that nearly didn't happen.

He and his wife, Andrea, and their dog, Tuffy, reside in Mt. Sidney, Virginia, only 23 miles from the Lincoln Homestead.

The Lincoln Homestead, in Rockingham County, Virginia, was built about 1800 by Jacob Lincoln, great-uncle of President Lincoln. Efforts are underway by the Lincoln Society of Virginia (www.lincolnva.org) to acquire and restore it. The residence stands only a few hundred yards from the Lincoln Family Cemetery, resting place for five generations of Virginia Lincolns.